A Book
of
Jean's
Own!

⌀ the ONION®

presents

A Book
of
Jean's
Own!

*A Collection of Wit, Wisdom,
and Wackiness from* The Onion's
Beloved Humor Columnist

Jean Teasdale!

Doodles by
Jean Teasdale!

Additional material by
Hubby Rick Teasdale!

 St Martin's Griffin ⋈ New York

For Patrick Swayze

THE ONION PRESENTS A BOOK OF JEAN'S OWN!: ALL NEW WIT, WISDOM, AND
WACKINESS FROM *THE ONION*'S BELOVED HUMOR COLUMNIST. Copyright
© 2010 by Onion, Inc. All rights reserved. Printed in the United
States of America. For information, address St. Martin's Press, 175
Fifth Avenue, New York, N.Y. 10010.

www.stmartins.com

ISBN 978-0-312-64268-6

First Edition: October 2010

10 9 8 7 6 5 4 3 2 1

Contents

Contents

Contents

Foreword
by Hubby Rick Teasdale

SO HERES JEANS BOOK. Go NUTS.

Preface

You hold in your hands the first-ever humor-oriented offering of Onion Books, the publishing arm of Onion, Inc., the world's largest media empire. Known for publishing volumes of reprints of its renowned newspaper parent, *The Onion*, and its venerable *World Atlas*, Onion Books is now making the plunge into fare of a more lighthearted sort. For its inaugural leap into the realm of rib-tickling, it has chosen, quite fittingly, Jean Teasdale, *The Onion's* veteran humor and human-interest columnist.

What makes Jean so enchantingly unique is that, unlike most of us, she possesses a funny bone for a brain. And what a thick funny bone it is! For nearly two decades in *The Onion's* back pages, our resident comedienne has shown us that there's a lot to laugh

at from everyday life, whether it's being fired multiple times from minimum-wage jobs or being cursed with a cumbersomely huge body. Readers who love getting their regular Jean "fix" tell us that her columns are just the thing for when they need a reminder that their lives could be a lot worse.

Whether you're already a fan, or a first-time pilgrim to the Sage of Blossom Meadows Drive, we have no doubt that Jean's humorous adventures and observations will no doubt strike a chord amongst those who don't wish to have their existing worldview challenged.

To borrow Jean's personal motto, "Keep smiling!"

Judith Karst-Zweibel
President, Onion Books

Acknowledgments

Without crucial support and inspiration, the dream that was *A Book of Jean's Own!* would have never come true. I owe an enormous debt of gratitude to:

My two precious kitties, Priscilla and Garfield. You have given me countless hours of unconditional love and bottomless compassion. It is a great honor to be both your best friend and mommy.

My buddy Fulgencio, a longtime pal whose "You go girl!" exhortations of support have helped me in ways he'll never know. He is literally an angel. No, really! I've seen him wear a pair of angel wings when he goes on a night on the town with his male friends who like to wear dresses! Fulgencio is an F.O.J. (Friend of Jean!) of the highest order!

These following people and things, in no particular order: Kate Palmer, sunshine, Marc Resnick, chocolate!!, Dan Greenberg, bunnies' noses, Julie Smith, love, David Reynolds, snuggles, Mike Loew, the smell of babies, Scott Dikkers, daisies, Joe Randazzo, the color pink, Carlos Yu, magic, Peter Serafinowicz, unicorns, Rick Martin, laughter, Rebecca Bengal, raw cookie dough, John Krewson, doilies, Dan Guterman, polyester (an essential building-block for stuffed animals), *The Onion* writing staff, bubbles, Jack Schneider, scented air fresheners, Danielle Gale, glitter, Andrew Block, and baby ducks. (By the way, don't read anything into the order. The color pink is not necessarily more important than Rebecca Bengal, for example!)

And I would be amiss if I didn't save the biggest thank-you of all to my Jeanketeers. I don't know your names, or just how many of you there are, but were it not for you, I'd probably be stuck in some minimum-wage job somewhere. Actually, I still work in a minimum-wage job. I just wouldn't have my column, and my life would be much poorer for it. (Poorer in quality, not financially.)

Oh, all right, and I suppose I should thank my Hubby Rick Teasdale too, even though he's a great

big grouch most of the time. But even I must admit that without the hubby, my column would lack a lot of spark. Then again, it would make more room for references to kitten whiskers!

Smoochies,

Jean Teasdale!

May 2010

I'm Jean Teasdale, and I Have a Funny Way of Looking at Things!

Aren't introductions awkward? Don't get me wrong; I love meeting people and making new friends. I'm the type who will start up a conversation with a total stranger in a waiting room, a laundromat, an all-you-can-eat buffet, a movie theater, a juror room—you name it! However, when it comes to written introductions, I'm at a bit of a loss. For one thing, they stink! They sit there like bumps on a log and cry out to be skipped over. Intros just stall you from getting to all the fun action, the real meat of the book. Plus, they can be a real rhymes-with-witch to write! After all, how do I sum myself up in a few words, especially given the vast and colorful tapestry that has been my life?

Should I call myself an average, humble homemaker who lives at 1567 Blossom Meadows Drive, Apartment 4B? I could, but it would mean leaving so much out, because this homemaker has worn many hats in her day. It's true: If you live in my area, you've probably known me at various times as your supermarket cashier, your drugstore cashier, your liquor store cashier, your truck-stop waitress, your bowling-alley shoe booth clerk, your junior shampooist, your assistant florist-trainee, your soft-serve ice cream server, your advertising-flyer deliverer, your discount clothing-store sales associate, your indoor flea-market vendor, and your data-entry clerk. You may also know me as one of the Pamida's best customers. Or you may know me as the woman who dresses up in bunny ears every Easter and waves to cars from the balcony-porch of her apartment. For it's true, I am all those things.

I'm also known as the wife of a Mr. Richard Teasdale, better known to readers of my column as Hubby Rick. While I hold down the fort, Rick works full-time at a tire center. I guess you could call Rick my rock. Actually, Rolling Rock may be more accurate! Because he drinks a lot of beer, get it? (See how this is a humor book?) Rick and I have been together nearly twenty years, through thick and thin and good days and bad. I

The hubby himself!

ask you, how many shotgun marriages can say the same? Sure, neither his dad nor my mom were thinking much about the long term when they caught us making whoopee in the back of Rick's rusted-out Chevy Luv in the Jewel parking lot all those years ago—they just wanted to make an honest man out of him, at least until they could talk the church into an annulment. But I guess Rick and me are like two old shoes—except I'm a fuzzy slipper and Rick is a steel-toed boot! Whatever our differences, I can't imagine being with anyone else. It would take heaven and earth to pry this ring off my finger—well, maybe just Dean Cain! (Hubba hubba!)

Sadly, I can't say that I'm a Mommy Jean as well as a Wifey Jean. Personally, I think being a mother is the greatest job on earth (personal shopper is a close second). But something's always been in the way—namely, our tummies!! Just kidding ...well, kind of. Rick's boys swim, there's no doubt about that—it's just that they seem to prefer pickling in Coors than baking in my toasty little baby oven! Anyhow, never say never—there's still plenty of ticking left in my biological clock!

the this T.M.I.??

Look for my witty and wacky "Jean Proverbs" throughout this book!

The other grand passion of my life (it may be my only grand passion) is that delectably sweet, rich, brown food of the gods that has for so long served as my muse, savior, and mid-day snack: yep, none other than almighty chocolate! I shudder to think of a world without it. I love all kinds of yummy chocolate concoctions, many of my own invention!

Ooey, Gooey Choco-Cocoa-Mocha-Mint Raspberry Cupcakes with Coconut-Caramel Icing, anyone? Then again, I'm the type to get a contact high from a discarded Hershey's Kiss wrapper! With chocolate, who needs marijuana and cocaine? Actually, lots of people. Still, I'll take a chronic addiction to chocolate to a semi-truck full of OxyContin any day! (I am also extremely addicted to coffee.)

For many women, marriage, chocolate, and an endless string of part-time jobs would be fulfillment enough. Not for me, though. Years ago, I realized I would need something more. I had always loved to express myself through writing, whether in my diary or compositions at school. (True, I never did better than a C-plus in English. But I still think it was the heart

in my work that mattered most, less so spelling, grammar, sentence composition, choice of subject matter, and ability to stay on point.) With writing, I could be totally honest, sincere, and original 'til the cows came home! And because I did it in my spare time, I didn't have to worry about parents, siblings, stepsiblings, aunts, uncles, teachers, priests, den mothers, bosses, or classmates peeking over my shoulder and "correcting" me. It was not only tons of fun, but more therapeutic than getting massaged on a fluffy cloud by a giant teddy bear! (Well, almost!)

Hand-in-hand with the writing comes something very valuable. Without it, my career would be a total wash. Not only am I a writer, there's another Jean you should know about: Jean the kidder. Yep, I'm a bit of a card—let's just say my funny bone takes up most of my arm! For example, how many people would ever think to wear a round red clown nose at their job? This one would! It's stuff like that that sets me apart from the crowd. Of course, I'm always asked by my supervisor to take the nose off, as it supposedly "bothers" the customers or makes my fellow co-workers "uncomfortable." And I comply, but hopefully I've planted the seed in people's brains that life need not be so serious. (You're welcome!)

Even if I can't always express my sense of humor

in public, it's far too good to keep to myself. So long ago I decided to join it with writing. I'm rarely without my notebook and something to write with, usually a six-color pen. (And yes, I use all the colors, even the hard-to-make-out orange!) Besides the crazy circus that is my life, I write down my thoughts, observations, or whatever darn thing that enters my head! Sometimes, when I'm on a real tear, I fill page after page. Does that happen to other writers? I'm not sure, but surely it must. I have heard of "writer's block," though. Not to brag, but I've rarely experienced that. I guess I must have some kind of God-given gift for putting pen to paper. And I'm not even counting margin doodles. I should have entered this book-writing business a long time ago.

You might not think that everyday life would provide any inspiration at all, but believe me, it does! Take my household clutter, for example. Boy, if that mound of laundry and old *Good Housekeeping* magazines could talk! (Actually, it has, and it's told me, "Feed me some more of those yummy tube socks and profiles of Kelly Ripa!") From "cultivating" science experiments in the fridge, to hunting for buried treasure between my sofa cushions (so that's where my iron and ham sandwich have been all this time!), my columns have shown that humdrum home life can be anything but! I

Note: I wrote this before I found out about "chick lit".

Casa Teasdale! (upper floor, second window from left)

don't limit my observations to the confines of my one-bedroom apartment, however. For example, ever notice that trying on clothing can itself be very trying? And did you know that the only thing I've improved on with age is aging? Oh, and men! Don't get me started! Pair this with my incredibly rare female perspective (seriously, there are not enough gals out there telling it like it is!), and you get literary dynamite! Sure, maybe you uninitiated aren't used to a sassy mama dishing it out, but if I don't do it, who the heck will?

For me, laughter and life go hand in hand—and if you have a life like mine, you need all the laughter you can get! See, I'm the type of person whose parking place

gets stolen; who receives her order last at every fast-food joint she goes to, even if it's just a Pepsi; whose umbrella blows hopelessly inside-out the second she steps outside in the rain; who gets the evil eye from her fellow co-workers when she forgets to bring in a snack during her assigned snack day; who tears out the seam in the posterior of her leggings when she tries to wrest two carts apart at the supermarket; who gets the antenna broken off her car at least twice a year ...shall I go on? Okay! I'm also the one whose microwave implodes when she's nuking some much craved-for cheese nachos, and who, when she wears a button-down shirt, doesn't notice her middle button has been open all day, revealing her bra and cleavage to all the world!

Once in a while I get asked, with all the crazy stuff that happens to me, why don't I just dig a grave and lie in it? Well, I suppose I could, but it wouldn't really work in my favor, would it? I'm a firm believer in the notion that, if life gives you lemons, throw them out and make Crystal Light instead, because who needs the extra calories?!? See what I'm driving at here? It feels better to laugh at life than to cry, so why not opt for giggles rather than sobs? And if you're still not sure how to go about it, hopefully this book will show you.

I guess I'm just a daydreamer at heart, thinking of what should be rather than what is. It's true: If I'm doing something, chances are I'm thinking about something else entirely different. I'm not content to satisfy myself with the immediate present, because let's face it, reality is strictly for the birds! I do a lot of reflecting. You name it, I've probably reflected on it. Sometimes I just get lost in the unnoticed beauty in the patterns of ceiling tiles. I admit that this has sometimes gotten me in trouble at jobs. (A word of advice—never daydream and laminate at the same time!) Hubby Rick once asked me if there was some such thing as remedial special-ed classes for adults, because I could sure use them. (Hardee-har-har, Rick!) Well, call me a flake or a ditz all you want, but none of us were meant to be machines, and I firmly believe that if people were more in touch with their inner imaginations, they'd be a lot happier!

And think about it—maybe if there were more people like me, the world would be a lot easier to live in. True, we'd have to expect things like getting fired a lot from jobs, or accidentally tripping and falling over toddlers at the park, or losing teeth at our friend's wedding, but we'd greet it all with a wink, a smile, and a wistful sigh. And of course, if there were more people like me, there would be fewer people unlike me who

think people like me are completely out of our minds. Another plus!

So shrug off your cares, relax, and pamper yourself with this book! You deserve to!

(<u>R</u>eal chocolate kisses (from me to you!)

Don't Worry, It's Not THAT Kind of Book!!

Folks familiar with my column in *The Onion* are probably more than just a little stunned to see this. Yep, folks, it really is yours truly, Jean Teasdale, with her very own book!! Now, now, I know what some of you are thinking: "A book? Yeccch!" Well, let me put your fears to rest right away. Just because this book has lots of pages doesn't mean it's some boring old wordy slog. Not at all! In fact, you have my personal guarantee that what you're holding in your hands is highly readable and relevant—no *War and Peace* here! This is something I'd pick up at a bookstore without hesitation, and I am extremely selective! (Seriously—aside from the occasional self-help guide, *Red-book,* and mass-market paperback with an embossed butterfly on the cover, I'm a very tough sell on reading material of any kind.)

Having written for *The Onion* for twenty years (I started my career when I was a toddler! Ha!!), I've developed a pretty good sense of what my readers expect from me, and that is to laugh their cares away as they wrap their Snuggies close around them and savor their morning French vanilla coffee and chocolate-raspberry danish. You don't read one of my columns to be weighed down with a lot of unbearable emotional baggage—right, veteran Jeanketeers? I say, leave the drama to the daytime soaps—they pull it off better, anyway.

What's more, with this book, I've mostly done away with that "sequence" thing that often makes books a tedious pain to read. I'm not one of those snobby authors who expects you to read their books left-to-right, cover-to-cover. You can flip around this thing and read middle parts and end parts and it won't matter. You could even save this part for the very end and you won't really miss anything. Don't you love that? In a sense, the way I've structured my book is more realistic. Life is more like a series of little moments than big things that continuously happen and lead to something grand. When you experience something, it doesn't necessarily mean you've reached some kind of ending or resolution. Sometimes several things can happen to you at once, and none of them lead to anything permanent. When

something happens to me, it's not like I sail off into the sunset. Usually it just means that I have to get up early the next morning and go to work. I suppose in a way that could be sort of an ending. But even so, an ending doesn't last forever. Inevitably something happens after the ending, even if it's a whole lot of nothing. Okay, end of profundity! This is supposed to be a lite read, after all! Anyhow, as I said, skip around to your heart's content.

On top of its universal accessibility, this work of art is a humor book, too! But just so there's no confusion, my Jeancadets-in-training, this is all 100 percent squeaky-clean humor. I don't like the type of joking that hurts people. Life is too short to be mean-spirited. For example, I don't like humor that makes fun of people's appearances. As a woman of enhanced poundage (to put it in a classy way for once), I know what it's like to be the butt of mean jokes. I also never understood why some folks find it so funny when something nice is wrecked or someone gets hurt. What's so funny about taking a pie in the face? Be-

surefire mark of literary excellence!

sides being a waste of a scrumptious treat, cream and meringue in the eyes could potentially damage your eyesight. If I saw someone slip and fall on a banana peel, I would like to think that, instead of laughing my fool head off, I would immediately come to that person's aid, or possibly dial 9-1-1 on my cell phone if the person was seriously injured, making sure to not move him (or her) and placing a blanket or coat over the victim so he (or she) does not go into shock. Of course, try telling all this to one of those cheap radio "shock jocks"—you know, that guy (never a gal, if you've ever noticed) who loves to offend and humiliate people he doesn't even know. Well, those folks can have their bikini babes and gas-passing sound effects and seven-figure salaries. At least I have been given the unique opportunity to show people how humor really should be done: gently, easy-going, and 100 percent ridicule-free! (Well, okay, I admit I come down on Hubby Rick a bit. But he deserves it, as you'll see.)

Instead of mining the toilet bowl for jokes (eww!), I use as my inspiration the great newspaper humorists and columnists that I grew up with and who paved the way for my own career. I'm thinking, of course, of the late, great Erma Bombeck. Also, Art Buchwald, when he wasn't being political, Ann Landers, when I wanted

someone to tackle the truly hard stuff, and the "I'm not making this up" guy who writes in capital letters a lot. Not only did they make newspapers readable beyond the comics, they also showed that you can turn your fun hobby writing about ordinary life and stuff into a viable career! Well, in my case, semi-career. *The Onion* only pays me $40 per column. (No, it's never been adjusted for inflation.) In fact, I provide what my editor refers to as "filler." When they're a little short on editorial content, or they didn't sell enough ad space, plop goes a pre-written *Room of Jean's Own* onto the page, where it fits as snugly as chocolate around nougat (Mmmm)!

Okay, so I get paid peanuts and they only use my articles when they fit. But heck, I'm published, aren't I? Goes to show how a true labor of love can eventually pay off in a small way. Besides, money's near the bottom of the list of my priorities, believe me. Put another way, I love to sing, but "Dough-Re-Mi" is not in my repertoire! Also, I ask you: How many books have you read that are decorated with actual doodles by the author? It's soooo

Jean Proverb
#212

When life hands you a yeast infection, make BREAD!!!

intimate—almost like glimpsing into my notebook! Why isn't that done more often by these bestselling authors everyone thinks are so great? (I'm talking to you, Jacquelyn Mitchard!) Had I the time and budget, Jeanketeers, I would crochet book covers for every copy, complete with a handle and an attached pom-pom bookmark. That craft definitely needs to develop beyond just Bible covers.

Without years of dedication to what I believed in, this book would not exist. And yes, I am getting paid an advance for it. So what if, after taxes, it will pay off only part of my massive credit-card debt. Sure beats the heck out of court-ordered wage-garnishing, if you ask me!

I Am Jean Teasdale.

I am all around you.

I see the joy and beauty of life.

In even the most small and ordinary things.

I am the smell of rain in the air.

I am a daisy growing on the roadside.

I am a soap bubble bursting on a dog's nose.

A chalk hopscotch game on the sidewalk.

The reassuring, ever-present hum of a fluorescent light.

A playground swing that has slipped one of its chains.

I am the pilot light on a stove.

A toy koala bear dangling off a rearview mirror.

A sparrow nesting in the Pamida sign

I am a pair of XL panties on the bottom
of a clearance table.

A square of lint caught in the dryer lint trap.

A bag of chips stuck in the corkscrew spiral
of a vending machine.

I am a rainbow slick of oil in a rain puddle.

I am the frayed cord of a hair dryer.

A pant leg caught in a bike chain.

A bent hair pin.

The missing piece in a jigsaw puzzle.

The stuck wheel on a shopping cart.

I am the last remaining cheese puff in the barrel.

I am a really good ballpoint pen.

I am the cracked coffee mug the ballpoint pen is in.

I am a desk drawer.

I am a computer mouse.

I am a computer screen.

I am a computer keyboard.

I am Jean Teasdale.

Say It Loud and Proud—
"I Feel Sorry for Myself!"

Could somebody please tell me what's so wrong with self-pity? I don't know about you, but for me, feeling sorry for myself is like smearing Carmex on my chapped brain. By calling it a stigma, I fear we're missing out on an unexpected pleasure. Even the term "wallowing in self-pity" sounds perfectly peachy—reminds me of relaxing in a nice, warm bubble bath!

After all, if I don't feel sorry for myself, who will? Certainly not Hubby Rick—when he's not working, he's out getting wasted. My pal Fulgencio wants to "keep it fun" (his words). As for my family, forget it. They're far too self-involved to get involved in my self-involvement! My dad is a thrice-divorced shopping mall Santa whose whereabouts are currently unknown. When I call my

mom, she always mentions the $100 I still owe her for a roundtrip Greyhound bus ticket eighteen years ago. And, saddest of all, I don't have any children to confide in and give me reassuring foot rubs. So you can see how I have little choice but to cry on my own shoulder. Sure, it might look a little strange, but you have to work with what you're given. Am I right?

Jean Proverb #91

They shouldn't be called shopping malls, they should be called shopping MAULS!

If you're in the middle of a streak of bad luck, or you feel misunderstood or maligned in some way, don't be some stoic fuddy-duddy—just give in and self-indulge! And I'm mainly talking to you, ladies! Women are so good at feeling sorry for others. Our hearts go out to virtually anyone with a problem. Well, it's about time we directed some of that generous pity toward ourselves! Because if you think about it, we have a lot to feel sorry for ourselves for.

Self-pity needs to stop being taboo, and your old pal Jean wants to bring it smack-dab into the mainstream. If you feel sorry for yourself, don't hide it and don't fight it—surrender! Say it loud and proud! Call in sick. Stay

in your bedroom. Don't wash your hair or brush your teeth. Dressing down is an absolute must—wear your old, worn, but comfy nightshirt (my Tweety Bird one is my personal fave!), or just your undies. Play fun mind games with yourself. Pretend that you never existed *It's a Wonderful Life*–style, and envision the ways in which your family and friends would be deprived. Imagine revenge against people who have wronged you. Is this all mere bitterness? No way! In fact, it's sweeter than a peppermint patty! It's like muscle relaxant for the soul!

Now, don't worry, I'm not asking you to starve yourselves to death or deny yourself any contact with the outside world—far from it! A party is hardly a party without yummy snacks and entertainment and other creature comforts. When organizing a self-pity party, make sure you stock up on all your favorite snacks. I prefer a combination of the savory and sweet—cheese puffs (preferably the barreled variety, because they're easier to seal than bags and stay upright on the non-level surface of a bed) and of course, my trusted old standby, chocolate (good ol' reliable Hershey's normally, but sometimes Fannie May Trinidads, Reeses Peanut Butter Eggs, or Ferrero Rochers for special self-pity occasions, especially those that fall around the holidays, or after unexpected events like job firings). Watch TV

Oh, and don't forget the vodka!

shows and DVDs to your heart's content, preferably ones whose lead characters are heroic, misunderstood types who are ignored or mistreated (Lifetime Movie Channel is generally your best bet on this one).

The cardinal rule about self-pity parties is that you have to go it alone. It doesn't really work to invite people to your self-pity party; otherwise it becomes a plain old party. True, at a regular party, you can try to shift the focus onto yourself, and get all passive-aggressive with guests who have slighted you in the past, or put them on guilt trips for various things. But in general, self-pity is a bit too tricky to incorporate into a normal party. I guess it's because of all the distractions.

Besides, most parties with people only last an evening; a self-pity party can go on for days if you want—weeks, even! I've never done one for that long, but I did once spend nearly a week just floating, floating, floating on my waterbed, getting up only to go to the bathroom and eat chicken pot pies. (We keep a mini-fridge in the bedroom, and I moved the microwave in there, too, so I didn't have to go to the kitchen—clever, huh?) Sadly, the fun ended when Rick called 9-1-1. Leave it to Mister Insensitive himself to completely misread my intentions and send a squad of paramedics over! Long story short, we ended up owing a big,

and I've tried! →

fat $500 ambulance fee, and it was all I could do to persuade Dr. Plimm, my physician, from putting me in the psych ward. Apparently Hubby Rick isn't the only type of person who thinks that someone who wants to be in bed for six days is loco in the cabeza. I swear, Rick only did that to humiliate me! I think he only cared that the microwave wasn't in its usual spot. Really, Rick was the only downside to that whole experience. I felt just dandy!

So the next time, when something unfortunate happens to you, or you just feel like saying "poor little me" in a special way, take a cue from your old pal Jean and throw your very own self-pity party! You have my guaranTeasdale that you'll emerge from it feeling as relaxed, renewed, and revitalized as from any expensive day at the spa!

Now, may I also ask what is so all-fired awful about the concept of "coasting through life"?

What's Better than Sex? Well, I'll Tell You!

I was inspired to do this list as I was making my patented "Better Than Sex" Cocoa Brown Sugar Caramel Brownies with Hazelnut-Mint Glaze. I had once heard the expression "better than sex" used to describe a sinfully tasty treat, and decided to "adopt" it for my own use. But then I thought, hey, wait—isn't eating in general better than sex? Well, of course it is. Then that led me to think about the dozens and dozens of other things that are better than sex—so many that I got distracted and poured half a cup of baking soda into the brownie batter! Yuck!

But come on, admit it—TONS of things are better than making whoopee. Answer me this: If sex is so great, why is it so many people have other things on their minds when they're doing it, like what they're go-

ing to have for breakfast in the morning, or wondering what that schmutz is on their pillowcase? Don't tell me that never happens! Anyway, here's my list of the 20 greatest things that are better than sex. (I originally came up with 161, no big chore, but the hard part was paring them down to the very best just for you!)

Twenty Things that Are Better than Sex

A rainbow after a rainstorm.

The feeling you get after finishing a project you've put off for a long time.

Finding $10 in a coat pocket.

Leftover cookie batter or frosting!

The first day of the year when your glasses don't fog up as you come in from outside.

A sudden cool breeze on a stiflingly hot afternoon.

The feel of a stuffed animal against your cheek.

An empty parking spot mere feet from
the mall's main entrance!

Discovering a long-lost earring.

The warm, fragrant scent of clean socks
just out of the dryer.

3-for-1 Fajitas Nite at Cactus Bill's!

Suddenly seeing a hot-air balloon in the sky.

A snow day!

Ice cream soup.

An all-day *Knots Landing* marathon
on SOAPnet.

Putting a hat on your cat!

Candlelight.

A cozy afternoon nap.

Scratching an itch (NOT in a dirty place!).

Polarfleece.

Lovin' from Jean's Oven

No. 1:
"Better Than Sex" Cocoa Brown Sugar Caramel Brownies with Hazelnut-Mint Glaze!

Oh please, would I mention this mouth-watering recipe in the "Twenty Things That Are Better Than Sex" chapter and then not share it you? The cruelty would be unconscionable! Trust me—if you make these brownies, you'll be wondering how a plate of fudgy-dudgy heaven could be so devilishly decadent at the same time!

Ingredients:

½ cup (1 stick) butter

1 cup unsweetened cocoa

1 tsp. vanilla extract

3 eggs
2¼ cups brown sugar, packed
¼ tsp. salt
1½ cups flour
20 caramels
½ cup half-and-half

For glaze:

8 tbsp. marshmallow creme
2 tbsp. water
⅓ cup brown sugar, packed
⅓ cup chopped toasted hazelnuts
⅓ cup finely chopped mint chocolate candies (such as Frango mints)

Preheat your oven to 325° F. Or just wait until a few minutes before you're about to pop the batter in— nooooo pressure! This is all about having fun.

Melt your butter in a saucepan, then pour into a large bowl. Add the unsweetened cocoa and stir until completely combined. Then add the vanilla, eggs, brown sugar, and salt, and beat. Once it's all mixed, add the flour.

Now set the brownie batter aside and turn your attention to the caramels and half-and-half. Melt the

caramels with the half-and-half in a double boiler, stirring constantly. Keep an eye on them and make sure they don't boil! Once completely melted, pour the caramel goo into the brownie mixture and mix thoroughly. Pour into a greased, 8-inch square baking pan and bake for 45–50 minutes, or until brownies are firm but still slightly gooshy in middle.

We're not done yet! While the brownies bake, prepare the glaze. In a saucepan on medium heat, stir together the marshmallow creme, water, and brown sugar. Add the hazelnuts and the mint chocolate candies, and stir until it's all one big, brown, nutty, minty mass, melted and heated through but not boiling. Spread glaze across the still-warm brownies, then cover and refrigerate for about an hour.

Once cool, cut the brownies into 2-inch squares and enjoy. Or just enjoy one 8-by-8 inch square—what the heck, you deserve it! Trust me, after this experience, you'll never have sex again!

(sorry for all the dirty dishes, but they're worth it!)

The Name Game

I've been thinking a lot about names lately. Like, why are some of us named Mildred and some of us Brandi? No offense to the Agathas and Ediths of the world, but why would your parents give you an ugly old-fashioned name when there are much, much cuter ones that would look fantastic on a birth certificate or crib headboard? Like Jenni and Jessi and Kathi and Lyndi and Lori and Kelli and Kristi and Wendi and Merri? You know, names that signify fun, bubbly, and carefree. They make the tongue literally jump for joy, because it doesn't have to gag itself on saliva (gross!) pronouncing something harsh or phlegmy. In fact, I'll go so far as to say that if your name ends with an "i" or an "ie," you're pretty much guaranteed a great life.

At school, I always noticed how girls with cute names tended to have the coolest clothes, the most friends, and the highest popularity. (Our homecoming queen was named Shanni, and she went on to be a successful realtor in our area.) I think the Kerris and the Candis of the world will back me up on my theory. I don't know if there's anyone named Iiii (pronounced "Eee-eee"), but if there is, she has to be the happiest person on Earth!

Granted, sometimes these girls could be kind of spoiled, even a tad rhymes-with-itchy, probably because they were treated like princesses for their entire childhoods. But it wasn't hard to imagine why: They clearly meant the world to their moms and dads, who, from the moment Mr. Stork arrived, wanted to spare their daughters the lifelong pain of having a long, embarrassing, hard-to-pronounce name. I remember this popular girl Missi used to go around checking if the less popular girls who wore jeans to school had made sure to straighten out the interior of their front pockets right after putting them on. She'd actually stop them in the hall and carry out an inspection if she suspected them of slacking. If their pockets were still all bunched up (you could tell if they had a hard time slipping their hands into their pockets), they caught some real

h-e-double-hockey-sticks (I know firsthand!). Is it normal to care about stuff like that? I suppose, since all the kids acted like Missi was the greatest thing since Madonna! Now imagine if Missi had been named Grizelda instead. She wouldn't have been nearly the superstar she was.

I know, you're thinking, "Envious much, Jean?" Well, count me as an honorary member of the Cute-Name Club, because since I was knee-high to a pair of knee-highs, my dad has called me "Jeannie." But it's only my nickname, not the name I was born with, and I think that has something to do with the way my life has gone. I've been within grasp of the brass ring more than a few times (I almost got a job at Claire's once, to name just one example!), but I always end up tumbling off the carousel horse. Maybe if I had been baptized a Chrissi or Missi, things would have a lot been different.

YEAH YOU WOULD OF BEEN A HOOKER — RICK

Rick is just jealous because all these girls turned him down!!

To complicate matters further, my middle name didn't exactly do anything to counteract the plainness of my first name. When I was born, my parents gave me the name Jean Meleanne. Meleanne? An interesting choice, you must be asking. Was that a traditional

family name? Were my parents' best friends named Mel and Leanne? Was it a play on "melons," their favorite fruit? Or a tribute to their faithful old melamine dinnerware set?

Heck to the capital N capital O! My middle name is not pronounced "Mel-Leanne." Instead, it's meant to be the name Melanie. My parents didn't know for certain how to spell "Melanie," and this was the closest they could figure. Ah well, they could have done worse— they were just off two letters. That's not bad for people who only write checks, sweepstakes entry blanks, and Christmas cards. Of course, my parents (they're named Horvel and Lillian, by the way) could have avoided the mistake by consulting a baby-name book or asking one of the nurses in the obstetrics ward, but who am I to judge? Parents have so much on their plate as it is, a daughter's misspelled middle name amounts to a piece of spit-out gristle! I know because my mom told me this during one of our screaming matches. I was plenty devastated at the time (I was 17), but through the years I eventually arrived at her hard-won wisdom. Same with my old selfish assumption that my dad was out getting crocked at the supper club every night—truth be told, he owned a roofing

company, and he had to wine and dine his clients to get business. Recognizing your parents' sacrifices is part of the maturing process.

Long story short, my parents never went back and changed the birth certificate, and I can't afford the court fees to change it anyhow, so I've learned to embrace my middle name for the charmingly unique thing it is!

Jean Proverb #801

Let's just say my rendezvous with French-cut panties produced a lot of "Uggggh-la-las" from Hubby Rick!

In fact, one day back in the eighth grade, I signed my homework assignments "Mel" instead of my regular old "Jean" because I thought it sounded spunky in a tomboyish way. For a few class periods, none of my teachers noticed. But then in pre-algebra class we took a pop quiz, and the teacher happened to look down at our collected papers and noticed that I'd written in a different name, and he asked me about it in front of everyone. I was forced to explain I was trying out a new nickname, and everybody snickered like it was the weirdest thing they ever heard. "Why do you want people to call you the same name as Alice's boss?" one girl asked with a sneer (her name was Wendi). So then for the rest of the week

people started calling me "Mel," then "Mel's Diner," then "Kiss mah grits, Mel!" By the end of the second week it had developed into "Vic Tayback," and that one pretty much stuck until the end of the school year.

Actually, now that I think about it, even if I did have a first name that ended in "i" or a properly spelled middle name, it's likely none of it would have made my last name sound any better. I've been a Teasdale for so long, I sometimes forget how much I wanted to forget my maiden name. Of course, my dad felt the exact opposite. "There's nothing wrong with the name of Speidr," he would tell my brother and me.

That's right, I started life as Jean Meleanne Speidr. Pronounced just the way you're thinking. "Your great-grandfather carried it all the way from the little town near the Austrian-Swiss border where he was born," my father often told us. "He refused to change it, even if it meant far better opportunities for him and his family." My dad loves our last name. He's also very proud of his first name, which he said his mother received in a dream while she was pregnant with him. In fact, at one point he had business cards made up that read "The Only Horvel Speidr in the State!" When we were kids, he hung a carved mahogany sign near our front door that read "The Speidrs' Web." Well, that took

a long time to live down. None of the neighborhood kids ever dared to come over to our house, because it was "filled with Speidrs!" Dad was Daddy Long Legs, and Mom was the Black Widow (not entirely inaccurate!). Me? I was Charlotte A. Cavatica. My brother Kevin didn't have a nickname. Maybe the kids simply ran out of spider names, but I suspect it was because he was the sole neighborhood supplier of illegal fireworks and trucker stimulants and they couldn't afford to get on his bad side.

I won't go so far as to say I married Rick to rid myself of an embarrassing maiden name, but I gotta admit, it sure was a big perk! "Teasdale" is very charming, I think. It gives me visions of a family of happy bunnies enjoying tea in a beautiful sunny green valley. It doesn't necessarily have to be bunnies, mind you—that's just what immediately comes to mind. It could be hedgehogs, too.

So while I'm content with being called Jean Meleanne Teasdale, I can't help dreaming up some new monikers for myself, just for fun. Would I have been more successful were I a Lindsi Windermere Teasdale? Would you talk to me more if I was a Kimberli Piper Teasdale? How about Mallorie Bree? Or Lexi Wylie? Sydnie Chablis? But it may interest you to know that

I, like the kitties in the kitty poet guy's poem that got made into a musical, have given myself a name that only I myself know and will never confess. Sorry, Jeanketeers, but it's a name that you will never guess. Oh, all right, it's Marjorie Snugglemittens.

Dreamin' of That Dream Day Job

I haven't yet found my life's part-time calling, and it's starting to nag me a tad. I thought that with my natural lack of ambition, I was a sure shoo-in for a great 20-hour-a-week, no-brainer gig. But no, everything I've done has had to involve hard work, extra hours, and knowledge. Remember that *I Love Lucy* episode when Lucy made chocolates? Or that old comedy movie in which the little man with the Hitler mustache only had to twist some bolts for his job? Where are those dream jobs?

As I mentioned before, your pal Jean is quite the career girl, though not by choice! Blame my parents for that. No sooner was I old enough to start earning money that they began pushing me out of the ol' homestead, demanding I get the proper "real world" experience to,

♡ **40** ♡

as my mom put it, "shake those silly daydreams out of your brain." "You can't count on Prince Charming to come to your rescue, especially a girl who puts away as many crullers as you do," she'd tell me. (Mommie Dearest? More like "Mommie Fearest!") But so far, nothing has been a perfect fit, and in my dark-cloud moments (and yes, I do have them!), I begin to wonder if the world is conspiring against me to keep me from achieving my dreams!

Like, sometimes, I'll get hired at a new job, only to discover that some of the work I'm required to do isn't even on the job description. Here's what I mean. Once I got a job at a pet store. When I first applied, the job

Jean Proverb #55

So exactly how much is an "oodle"?

duties were described as working at the cash register, stocking shelves, and feeding and watering the pets. All of that was true. But the description said nothing about cleaning dead cricket bodies out of the iguana's cage. This is what I'm talking about, Jeanketeers! Employers need to let you know about these things before you apply for jobs. Otherwise they have no right to be

shocked or complain when an employee runs into the customer bathroom bawling, or sits at their work stool plucking out their forearm hairs.

At another place, where I did data entry, I was sprung with the dreadful surprise that I had to know how to type with more than two fingers, and fast, too, even though, once again, it was not on the job description! (When I asked her about it later, my supervisor only replied that keyboard skills "were a fundamental requirement." College know-it-all!) I did take a typing class in high school, and I know that you're supposed to lay your fingers on the "home keys" and work from there, but I could never get the hang of looking away from the keys as I typed. I've just stuck by my tried-and-true index-finger method—I still have to hunt around a little, but generally get by by avoiding tricky keys like the semicolon and the back-slash, and the numbers, too. Anyhow, my perfectly reliable technique wasn't good enough for the folks at old SouthCentral Insurance. Apparently I was one of the slowest workers on our floor (they timed us in person—soooo much pressure!). Sheesh! I was always on thin ice at that place.

Well, I don't mean to sound like such a Gloomy Gloria—in truth I have many, many job strengths! For one thing, I'm a very talented gift wrapper. I just have

Tips for Coping with a Job You Dislike but Must Keep

When you can, spend time in your car— For breaks and lunches, your parked car is a great way to escape the pressures of your job. There's a lot more privacy and fewer critical eyes around when you need to collect your thoughts, space out, or not hyperventilate. The only downside is that sometimes the urge to switch on the ignition and drive away forever is too great. (That's how I left a job cleaning offices.)

Daydream a lot—This is a double-edged sword, I admit. Sometimes fantasizing is the only way to cope with boring and dreary work. But you can get caught doing it really easily. You do not want your boss shouting, "Hey, you, stop thinking about Ridge on *The Bold and the Beautiful* and get back to work!" (Boy, it's weird how psychic bosses can be sometimes!) Still, I can't tell you how many times my old standby, skipping along Willy Wonka's chocolate river hand-in-hand with Fabio (double-drool!), has gotten me through some seriously dull stretches!

Treat yourself to goodies sold near your work-place—Every time I get a new job (often), I always have to buy things at the stores nearby. It's a good incentive to keep working at a job I might otherwise quit or eventually get fired from. I'm pretty sure I stayed as long as I did at a mailroom job at a mortgage-lending firm because there was a great bakery across the street. Of course, during those four months, I managed to gain twenty pounds!

Keep a running list of things that remind you why you're better than a nasty coworker—Once in a while at a job, I've been known to, well, get on someone's bad side. Certainly not intentionally, but sometimes I encounter someone who has a lot of problems with my occasional lack of punctuality or teeny-weeny slip-ups. It's unfair, but it happens. To keep from getting really down about it, I always try to keep in mind what positive qualities I have that he or she sorely lacks. Things like empathy, a sense of humor, a bigger imagination, and the ability to recognize my mistakes as being part of what makes us human. Keeping a written list is also a good way to prepare yourself in case your supervisor calls you in to explain yourself if something unpleasant happens (like, accidentally shredding every copy of the most current employee-benefits manuals because you thought they were on the shred pile, to name a random example). Just make sure you keep that list on your person, or you can get into mucho agua caliente!

a good eye for knowing exactly how much wrapping paper an item needs. I'm also super at folding. At the Fashion Bug, I was the unofficial Chief Folder of the merchandise during the hours I worked! Also, I have an uncanny knack for arranging items on shelves so that they look fuller than they really are. That makes me perfectly suited for jobs at discount stores and supermarkets. And when food is involved, like in a restaurant or a supermarket, I'm really good at not eating on the job. (Don't let my pleasant plumpness fool you!) When I was assigned to the salad bar at Rax, I never, ever popped a single salad fixing in my mouth, even though there were literally dozens of buckets of mushrooms and olives and cherry tomatoes and croutons laid out before me ripe for the picking!

There's more! I'm extremely punctual for shifts that start after 10 a.m. I like to think I am well organized. I don't know for sure, because I've never had a workspace I was allowed to keep my stuff in overnight, but I can't imagine it's too hard to manage paperwork, as long as you're given file cabinets and folders to keep it in. Plus I have great communication skills. I'm really pleasant on the phone—I love talking to customers! Except when they're irate. Then sometimes I lose my head a little and start to cry.

And perhaps best of all, if I'm working in retail, I'm often that store's best customer. I've been known to spend two-thirds of my take-home pay on merchandise I found irresistible! And, if I happened to be issued a store credit card, sometimes I even owed money! Hubby Rick used to get on my case about that, but if you think about it, isn't it a good thing if employees buy a lot from the store they work for? It shows they believe in the store's fundamental mission—to offer things to people to buy—and aren't there just to do a day's work.

My friend Patti, who teaches old people at the local community college, says that I already found my real calling—writing—and that I should consider going back to school and getting a teaching degree so I can show others how to write. But I can't imagine doing that, because I hate school. Or more accurately, I hate what school has become. I was never big on doing homework, and have no reason to believe I've changed, so I don't know how I would get a degree. Plus, if I had to teach actual students, I'd be such a softie that I'd probably be forced to turn in my teaching badge! I'd hold class outside on every day that wasn't raining or snowing, and buy my students sodas at the student union, and pass everyone automatically—heck, I'd be handing out As like supermarket coupon flyers! Inevitably this would

land me in trouble with some uptight, humorless dean. But what can I say, I believe life should be fun and that everybody should get to succeed! Ah, if only more people believed in the beautiful world that I envision.

Right now I'm working five hours a day at my buddy Fulgencio's stall at our local indoor flea market. He calls it "¡Basura Fabulosa!"—"Fabulous Trash!" in Spanish. The work is divine—few crowds, plenty of time to catch up on the *Good Housekeeping* issues I've missed, and I'm surrounded by lots of lovely flea-market eye candy, like homemade quilts and tiny wicker doll chairs and American flag-shaped everything! It would come darn close to being my dream day job, save for one small hitch: I only get paid $20 a day. I'm also entitled to ten percent of each sale, but seeing as we mostly sell stuff like back issues of *Good Housekeeping* and VHS cassettes of Jean-Claude Van Damme movies, all I can say is, thank heavens for that $20!

Here's how I envision my dream day job:

• I work at a place that is busy enough to make the time pass quickly, but I never feel rushed or over-whelmed.

• If it's retail, I get a minimum 50 percent mer-chandise discount. This is soooo important.

• I sit on my very own chair.

• If the employee lounging area is outdoors, it has shade. (Preferably not shade provided by the Dumpster.)

• The vending machine contains Tato Skins, my all-time favorite potato chip. (Whatever happened to them, anyhow?)

• If I have to stock merchandise, it's light stuff (like cotton balls or stuffed animals) and I don't have to climb more than two feet off the ground. (I'm prone to vertigo.)

• Friendly coworkers who aren't great big Judge Judys about everything. You know what I'm talking about? Their tongues don't go all a-wagging just because you forget it's your turn to bring in the weekly treat, or, while distributing the mail, you somehow misplace the employees' payroll checks and everybody searches for them, then, at the end of the day, the office supervisor finds them in a bathroom stall under a copy of *Us Weekly* that you left on top of the toilet during your break.

• It taps into all my aforementioned strengths. To recap, that's wrapping, folding, arranging, not eating the merchandise, punctuality after 10 a.m., talking, and buying things.

See? I've never asked for much. So if you're an employer, and you think you have the ideal job for me, let

me know! It's a win-win situation for us both—me for obvious reasons, and you for the fact that you'd have a nationally recognized newspaper columnist manning your cash register or stocking your cotton balls!

JEAN MELEANNE TEASDALE
1567 Blossom Meadows Drive, Apt. 48B

jteasdale@theonion.com

OBJECTIVE:
To have so much fun it doesn't seem like work, and get paid doing it!

SUMMARY OF QUALIFICATIONS:
Years (exactly how many available upon request—a lady doesn't admit anything that would indicate her true age!) of experience in feature-column writing and opinion-having.

Years (again, exactly how many available upon request!) of customer service experience in retail and the private sector. Ability to deal with customers in various situations, provided they are nice and in a good mood.

Can laminate to some degree.

Am generous in heart and spirit.

I've also been told that I have very cute penmanship!

♡ **49** ♡

EDUCATION:
Gus Grissom High School, Class of 1989

WORK EXPERIENCE:
1990–Present
Columnist, *The Onion*
Disclosing intimate aspects of my life in columns of 500–800 word length; bringing a smile to the face of countless *Onion* readers; imparting insight with a sassy spark. Mastered meeting deadlines and writing complete sentences. In 2004, came in eighth for "Favorite Regional Columnist" in local free weekly *Pressing Matters*' annual Readers' Poll. In 2010, released my first-ever full-length book, *A Book of Jean's Own!* (Exclamation point part of the title, not the sentence)

Jan. 2006–Present
¡Basura Fabuloso! Booth Worker, Riverside Indoor Flea Market
Sell secondhand knickknacks, framed pictures, VHS tapes, and back issues of *Good Housekeeping*, *Cosmopolitan*, *Woman's World*, and other magazines. Other duties include loading and unloading merchandise on and off tables; arranging merchandise in attractive ways; using basic arithmetic skills; using a calculator; and occasional price negotiation with customers. On weekends, frequently shop yard sales or assist my friend/boss, Fulgencio Moreno (reference provided upon request), in picking up and transporting items he has purchased for sale. Occasional Dumpster-diving.

Dec. 1998–Continuing (Christmas season only)
Gift-Wrapper, Northway Mall
Cover gifts of varying size in wrapping paper. Skills involve cutting, taping, folding, and estimating accurate measurements under significant time restraints and customer pressure. Received very nice letter of recommendation from wrapping-booth supervisor, available upon request.

March–July 2005
Manager, Off-Season Santa
Ordering and stocking miscellaneous Christmas merchandise; dressing as elf and the Adorable Snowbelle (play on Abominable Snowman); helping owner/father Horvel Speidr, an authentic professional shopping-mall Santa Claus, get into and out of his special off-season Santa outfit (no easy feat); maintaining festive Christmasy appearance of store all year-round (in theory, as we closed after only four months due to a devastating fire); some bookkeeping.

September 2000–June 2002
Sales Associate, Fashion Bug
Selling trendy fashions at discount prices. Duties included cash register, folding and arranging merchandise on floor, fetching different sizes for customers in fitting room, assisting in bi-annual inventory, and cleaning the employee's bathroom when the housekeeping service didn't show up, which happened a lot, possibly because we were stuck in this mini-mall in a kind of run-down part of town.

May 1998–December 2001
Data Entry Clerk, SouthCentral Insurance
Entering numbers off big thick ledgers onto computer spread-
sheets; investigating and reconciling numerical variations and
miscellaneous written inconsistencies; and other duties I don't
quite recall because I held this job a while ago. Not really my
life's calling, but shows I can use an adding machine and work
with office spreadsheet programs if forced to.

February 1995–August 1997
**Customer Service Representative, Little Miss History
Dolls & Stories**
Worked in call center of extremely popular doll manufacturer.
Handled many types of customer service calls including sales,
returns and exchanges, and complaints (yes, a few people
actually complained about Little Miss History Dolls, which is
a very sad commentary on our society). Duties included call
transferring, situation resolving, headset wearing, and talking to lonely people during the third shift, who often seemed
to have Southern accents for some reason. Duties never
included product-testing and doll play, unfortunately.

More, much more, work experience available upon request!

Jean's Letters to God

Dear God,

Do you still have a long white beard, or are You now clean-shaven to reflect the times?

Love,

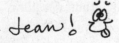

Jean!

Dear God,

Of all your angels, who's Your favorite? Do You prefer the fearsome adult ones with flaming swords, or the cute little cherubs?

Love,

Jean!

Dear God,

 If You are everywhere, as we are taught, take some friendly advice from Your ol' daughter Jean: You should probably stay out of our dirty-clothes hamper! (Actually, I suppose it's "Godforsaken" anyway, so You probably already know about it!)

Love,

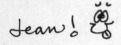

....

Dear God,

 I hope You like the Precious Moments nativity scene I set up for Christmas! True, I'm still missing the Baby Jesus, a couple of the camels, and Joseph, though a plain old shepherd is a decent substitute for him. But I will get them as soon as I can afford them. Actually, they phased out the camels so they're hard to find now, but I'll keep combing eBay. Tell Jesus I say Happy Birthday! Actually, You can tell Yourself that, too, can't You?

Love,

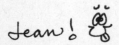

Dear God,

Did Jesus love overweight people, too? I'm sure He must have, but there's no specific mention of overweight people in the Sermon on the Mount. Unless there were plenty of "pleasantly plump" people back in Biblical days and everyone considered it the norm, so it didn't really matter.

Love,

Jean!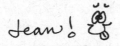

....

Dear God,

What's the best way to get pizza grease out of the carpet? Hubby Rick managed to drop a slice behind the sofa and I just noticed it today when I found my cat Garfield wedging himself underneath to lick it.

Love,

Jean!

....

Dear God,

If you give Hubby Rick and me a baby, I promise I'll stop eating erasers. I know I've been doing it since I

was a kid and it's a hard habit to break, but I vow that I will overcome it if I'm given an incentive.

Love,

Jean!

....

Dear God,

Were you as confused by *2001: A Space Odyssey* as I was? Was that big black thing meant to be You?

Love,

Jean!

....

Dear God,

Remember the other day, when Hubby Rick and I were watching the news, and there was a story about a girl from the Oriental country born with two faces, and Rick said, "There's proof right there that there is no God, because what God would be f-----d up enough to create that?" (I was going to omit the blasphemous part altogether, but since You see and hear everything anyway, there's no point in leaving it out.) Well, I just wanted to apologize on Rick's behalf, because that was

out of line. I do not really understand why You created a baby with two faces, but I'm sure You had a good reason somewhere down the line.

Love,

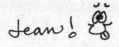

Dear God,

Can You create a cat that can live as long as a human? I've already lost one cat and my other ones are getting up there. I think You should let cats live longer to make up for the fact that bad people often live to an old age.

Love,

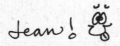

P.S. Please say hello to my kitty Arthur for me. I hope he is having a nice nap on his little cloud.

Dear God,

The other day Hubby Rick asked me where I was when the brains were passed out, and while I didn't think that was very kind of him to say, it got me to wondering: Could You make me smarter? I know I'm a little old to be finally getting around to asking this, but seeing as You are in charge of brains, don't You think, as a change of pace, it would be fun to give a grown woman some extra smarts? Wouldn't it be terrific if I woke up one day and could do calculus equations off the top of my head, or fix a car engine by myself? You know, something fun and unexpected. It would sure put Rick in his place, too!

I don't have to necessarily be a genius, either. I would even settle for having just enough brains to earn more money and live in a better neighborhood.

Just a thought!

(Hey, does having this thought make me smarter already? Maybe!)

Love,

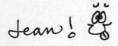

Feeling Blue?
Then Do the "Plush Jamboree"
with Jean!

Years ago, I came up with the following surefire way to battle the blahs! Make my "Plush Jamboree" a tradition in your own home—it's easy and tons of fun!

What you'll need:

Bed (preferably king- or queen-size, ideally a waterbed)
Stuffed animals, many
Yourself!
A fun attitude!

*First, start with a clean
bed with fresh sheets.*

*Second, pile all your
stuffed animals on the
bed. And I mean all of
them—you'll need as
many as you can find!*

*Now, off with
all your clothes!*

Lay down among your stuffed animals! (Or, if you think your bed can take the weight, kowabunga!!)

*Roll around over and over, letting your stuffed
animals tumble all over you! Savor the warmth and
softness of the synthetic plush! Does it tickle a bit in
the sensitive areas, too? Good! It should!*

*Take all the time in the world—the stuffed animals
don't mind (at least the ones that aren't underneath
you!). Roll over on your stomach and let the plushy
bliss wash over you. If you're on a waterbed, the waves
will gently rock you into a wonderful, tranquil heaven.*

If, I, Jean, could choose my death, it would be to die in my sleep, surrounded by the loving glass-eye gaze of my very best friends in the world.

P.S. When you do finally get up, make sure no one is sticking to you! It's embarrassing to be browsing at the mall and suddenly a stuffed frog comes tumbling out of your pant leg! (True story! Boy, I sure had a lot of explaining to do at the Hallmark store!)

Jean Teasdale
"Fun" Fiction, Part 1

E ver wonder what your life would have been like had it taken a slightly different path? I think about that "what if" stuff like all the time. But overall, I gotta say, I'm pretty happy with the way my life has gone. True, for all my years of work experience, your old pal Jean hasn't exactly shot up the corporate ladder (in fact, my foot barely touches the bottom rung!). And the only babies I'm a mommy to have fur and whiskers! (Mind you, parenting cats is a role I take very seriously, but it would've been nice to have a human baby by now, or two or three.)

But I choose to look on the bright side—I've evaded a lot of responsibilities, and consequently have less stress than most people of my generation. At least I'm not one of those career-obsessed workaholics who only care about

money, money, money and who worry themselves into an early grave because they refuse to sit back and smell the roses. You call that living? Frankly, I'd rather put up with the indignity of having a 19-year-old boss order me to retrieve from an alley Dumpster a cash-register tape I accidentally threw away than living a life of prosperity yet never, ever having a single moment of peace. Then again, maybe that's not much of a choice. Well, I'm going off the subject.

Anyway, just because I'm content with my life choices doesn't mean I'm not blessed with an imagination, and a big one at that! I often amuse myself by writing fun fiction about my life. (I know, you're probably asking, "Doesn't Jean mean fan fiction?" I do, but since I'm already my biggest fan anyway, it seems redundant!) This is a whole new side of me you haven't seen before in my columns. So kick back and enjoy some fun fiction as we imagine how my life would have been...

If Hubby Rick Had Been Hired for That Assistant Manager Position at the Tire Center!

Man, did my new Lexus LS run like a dream! It's funny—I never cared much about luxury-class vehicles before, but once I had one, I was a total sucker for their

incredible power and wonderful handling! I felt like I was driving a torpedo through a giant mound of Cool Whip! Hubby Rick was such a pussycat to give this to me for my birthday!

But know what was better than driving a Lexus? Being able to drive it into a heated three-car garage! Wow, just watching that garage door open at the touch of a button clipped to my driver's-side sun shade sent shivers down my spine! Gone were the days when my old Dodge Neon sat outside in the apartment parking lot all winter and practically froze into a carsicle through April!

And you know what was even better than driving a Lexus into a three-car garage? A three-car garage attached to a gorgeous six-bedroom McMansion in the toniest part of town! Finally, our years and years of living in tiny apartments a mouse would feel cramped in had come to an end! As I walked from the garage, through the spacious mudroom, and into our state-of-the-art kitchen, I felt like a queen!

I have to admit, as I gazed at our gleaming, stainless-steel Viking oven range, tears stood in my eyes. I always got a little misty when I recalled Hubby Rick's words back when he first told me he got the assistant manager position, now two years ago to the day: "Jean,

baby, now that I have this $6.50-an-hour wage increase and an extra five days of sick leave, you can finally live in the style in which you've always dreamed."

Rick had never been a talkative type—he keeps his emotions pretty close to his vest. Even I, his own wife, never knew until that happy day that his greatest ambition in life was to take me away from my life of drudgery. To my utter shock, my gallant hubby told me that he had never wanted me to work in the first place! "God didn't intend you to man cash registers and mop up toddler vomit from dollar-store floors," he said. "Too many people are unable to exercise their true talents. But you were meant to uplift people through your writings, which I have always secretly loved. [Another surprise!] Now you'll finally be able to devote your life to your greatest passions."

A few minutes later, Rick came home. Though it was only four o'clock in the afternoon, Rick's cushy job frequently allowed him to leave early. He no longer came home stinking of sweat and grease and dressed in motor oil-spattered clothes. Now he was resplendent in his crisp blue assistant-manager's coveralls, and his mustache was neatly trimmed and his hair combed neatly. If not for the coveralls, you would have thought he was a state senator.

We opted for an early dinner this day. I pressed a few wall buttons, and out popped our dinner-making robot, who whipped us up a mouth-watering pork tenderloin with boiled potatoes in mere minutes. The body-temperature-sensing automated-thermostat had adjusted the grand dining room to optimum comfort. I set the table with our best bone china, a (very) belated wedding present from my mother, who was thrilled to see her son-in-law finally make good. Thought it did take a little bit of adjustment at first, dressing for dinner had become second nature for Rick, and the feast on the table had some pretty tough competition from the feast on the eyes that was my very own hubby in a tailored tuxedo! And, embarrassed I am to admit it, I wore my diamond tiara during dinner. (Where else would it get use? Well, besides the many country-club soirées we commonly attended!)

After dinner, Rick and I retired to our master bedroom. (Hubba Hubba! No, the bedroom was really named "Hubba Hubba!" Rick had the words painted gold and hung over our door as a gift to me!) In contrast to the rest of the house, it was sparsely furnished, save for the super-sized luxury waterbed that took up nearly the entire room, and an 88-inch wall-mounted big-screen HDTV. Guests always seemed most in awe

of that room. But to me, the best part of the house was the other four bedrooms, which we had converted into multi-purpose rooms. There was my column-writing room; my Bedazzler room, where I did all my Bedazzling; a room for our two cats, with all the great toys, beds, and cat trees you could imagine; and my 365-day-a-year Christmas room. My very favorite bedroom of all, though, was completely empty. Let's just say we'd be shopping for nursery furniture just as soon as I began to show!

As our dinner-making robot brought our after-dinner beverages (Rick preferred a hot mulled wine; I still liked my good old Sleepytime Tea with a pinch of Equal!) the doorbell rang (opening strains of "Have You Never Been Lonely" by Olivia Newton-John). I said to just ignore it, but Rick said he should get up and answer it, because it could be some people soliciting donations for breast-cancer research. After his promotion, Hubby Rick became a lot more sensitive about the plight of those less fortunate. (By the way, did I mention that Rick received several more raises since his promotion, and was now making the unheard-of annual sum of—get this—$68,000?) I decided to accompany him downstairs, despite being in my peignoir.

The thick, oaken double-doors revealed none other

than Topher and Shanni West, our next-door neighbors. Yep, the very same Topher West, the golf whiz who took our high school all the way to state and later toured the semi-pro circuit, and the former Shanni Schuhheim, golden-girl-cheerleader-turned-star-realtor. They had a 12-year-old daughter named BrookeLynne who almost won a regional audition for a role on a Disney show. So this was a family that really had their act together.

Topher and Shanni were in the same grade as Rick and me, but we didn't exactly occupy the same social circles. Rick had been a jock, too, but Topher didn't consider a guy who warmed the bench on the wrestling team as his equal. At least, he didn't before. And Shanni didn't think it beneath her to sell us the very house she and her husband lived next door to; in fact, with the housing market bottoming out, she was more than happy to make a sale, even if it meant earning a much tinier commission!

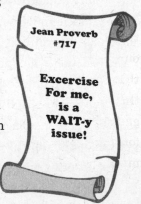

Jean Proverb
#717

Excercise
For me,
is a
WAIT-y
issue!

In fact, both Topher and Shanni looked like they had seen much better days. Topher wore the same pink button-down Lacoste alligator sweater I

remember him wearing back in high school, except now it was frayed and moth-eaten. His blond preppie haircut was thinning and laced with gray, and the years of tanning gave him some unsightly wrinkles. His broad smile revealed broken teeth as well as desperation. We soon realized that his arm was around Shanni not solely out of affection, but because she was having trouble supporting herself. Shanni had always been slender, but now she looked dangerously thin, and large bags hung under her lusterless blue eyes. It was as if some giant had placed them in a cardboard box for 15 years, like Barbie and Ken dolls his giantess daughter had grown out of, and, after the giant had finally decided to get rid of them, they had accidentally fallen out of the truck on their way to the St. Vincent de Paul for Needy Giants and wound up at our door.

Topher said they were out for an evening walk and thought they would stop by and say hello and ask how our new home was "doing" us. Perhaps he had forgotten that it wasn't really our "new" home, as we had lived there nearly two years, but I didn't correct him. Shanni gamely widened her dull, hollow eyes, though the effort must have been an incredible strain, and said how much she liked my peignoir. She then collapsed.

"I told Shanni not to exert herself!" Topher cried.

Rick gently scooped up Shanni—he picked her up from the front stoop like she weighed no more than a piece of tissue paper—and carried her to, appropriately, the fainting couch in our Victorian-style parlor.

Topher tearfully confessed that the real reason for their visit was that they had been evicted from their house and hadn't a dime to their name. Rather than ask for help, they had tried to act proud and "above it all," and keep up the appearance that they were still prosperous. But now they had nothing but the clothes on their backs and hadn't eaten for days. They had sent BrookeLynne to relatives, explaining that they were on an around-the-world cruise, but in fact they had no plans to take their daughter back because they simply couldn't afford her upkeep. Topher explained that they didn't expect charity. Instead, he said, all he wanted for the weakened Shanni was a chance to see the beautiful year-round Christmas room I had created. "It's the talk of the town, and I thought Shanni's last sight of this earth could be of that magical place," Topher said.

"Nonsense!" Rick said, clapping a brotherly hand on Topher's bony shoulder. "We'll put two cots in that room, and you can stay in there as long as you like. Our dinner-making robot will prepare a big meal for you and some nourishing broth for Shanni. You should

never be ashamed to ask for help if you need it."

"Really?" Topher queried, amazed. "Even after all our years of snotty, stuck-up behavior towards you and people like you, you, the Rick Teasdales, will take us in?"

"Of course!" Rick and I cried. And our dinner-making robot meeped in agreement!

And that's exactly what happened. Miraculously, the healing powers of the Christmas room proved to be real, as the very sight of its shimmering beauty not only soothed and revived Shanni but made her blue eyes once again shine like some kind of sparkling wine. Within a day she was eating solid food, and by the end of the week she was on her feet again. We also arranged to have BrookeLynne reunite with her parents, and there was not a dry eye in the house! Rick persuaded a society friend who owned an eight-hole golf course and driving range to take on Topher as his resident pro instructor. In time, Rick and Topher opened their own pitch-and-putt near the highway, and made a mint! It gave Topher and Shanni enough money to move into an even bigger and gorgeous McMansion.

Still feeling indebted to us, though they hadn't needed to, they invited us to live with them. We politely demurred, saying that our house may be smaller than

their new one, but it was home. Besides, it already held so many joyous memories of our now year-old baby daughter, and we wanted to make new ones!

Just think—none of it would have happened if Rick hadn't been hired for that assistant-manager job at the tire center!

Girl Power? Hook Me Up!

A h, the teenage years—braces, blemishes, and boys! (And I suppose "bosoms," too, though I prefer keeping things clean!) I'm sure I'm not alone in thinking they're years most people want to forget. My adolescence was, er, difficult, you might say. If you asked me what the worst day of my life was, I'd have to say it was one day when I was fifteen, when this bully Wendi snapped my rainbow suspenders against my, uh, bosoms (yeeowch!), someone dumped a fruit cup into my newsboy cap at lunch, I managed to get my perm so badly snagged in the temple piece of my glasses I had to cut it off with my social studies teacher's scissors, AND the gym teacher forced me to hang off a chinning bar for five whole minutes because he thought I was "faking" the fact I couldn't manage half a chin-up.

Also, when I came home, my mom was screaming at my dad about some "tramp," and I saw my older brother Kevin throw his old Pinewood Derby racer at our poor little dog Curlytop for going wee-wee on the carpet in his bedroom. And no one had made dinner, so I ate a popcorn ball left over from trick-or-treating a month earlier and it gave me a huge stomachache.

Then, after I fell asleep, I had that terrible recurring nightmare in which my bedroom crucifix came to life, and the little Jesus crawled down the wall and crept onto my bed and pried my mouth open and tried to force himself into it with his cold tiny brass hands. I always woke up before he succeeded, but that dream messed me up for years and years.

Sounds familiar, huh? Bet you can relate! But things will get better, a lot better, and that's what I want young, confused girls who happen upon this little book to understand. The pain and hard times don't last. Not to be a Lesley-Anne Downer, but I don't understand why some teens tragically decide to end their own lives when they are just a year or two away from co-signing on an apartment lease or buying their very first used car. Or perhaps others would not turn to drugs, or worse, shoot up schools or shopping malls, if they had only realized earlier that they could soon

serve on a jury. Oh, and did I mention no more sub-minimum wage? Yep, you'll be up to $6.55 an hour, just like us mature grown-ups!

Besides, this is the era of girl power. Because of it, today's girls are incredibly cool and practically invincible! Boy, do I wish I had some of that girl power when I was young. We had *Ms. Magazine*, but my mom wouldn't let me read it because she considered feminists sluts. If I had been born just a teeny bit later, not only would I have known that I could do anything a boy could, but I would wear cute clothes like pink high tops and hooded sweatshirts with a repeating kitty or bunny pattern on them. And I'd probably be able to rap.

Jean Proverb #800

Politics, schmolitics!!

Anyway, for those tween and teen girls who still haven't plugged into this fabulous girl power, your big sis Jean has a few choice nuggets of wisdom. Sure, I bet you think you're too smart to take advice from an old lady, but trust me, this wise owl knows what she's talking about!

Don't dye your hair or get your ears pierced. This might sound like a tall order, but trust me on this!

It's soooo important to be yourself. What's all the rush with looking like an adult, anyway? When I was 15, I was still styling my Barbie head's hair and playing with my Tree Tots Tree House. Why? Because even then, I knew that the magic of my youth wasn't going to last, and I wanted to squeeze in as much playtime whimsy as I could. So believe your old pal Jean when she says that adulthood is strictly overrated. Trust me—you'll have plenty of time for aging, dead-end, no-fun jobs, and quarrels with the hubby. On a related note...

Don't starve yourself. In fact, you should eat anything and everything while your metabolism can handle it! Believe it or not, once upon a time big sis Jean could eat her whole basket of Easter candy in one sitting and she wouldn't gain an ounce. Of course, I was nine at the time! Then, a mere year later, all the puberty hormones kicked in and I was constantly exhausted and my chest budded and it seemed to weigh more than half my previous total body weight. I never really recovered from that experience. So go ahead and indulge, girls! There's plenty of time to fret about weight and eating habits later.

Don't cut your arms and legs with a razor blade. That's just gross, and it leaves ugly scars. Never harm your beautiful young body! You'll get stretch

marks in many of these same places later anyway, so just consider those your flesh wounds.

Don't kill anyone!!! Seriously, don't do it! If you do, you be forever haunted by your terrible crime. Not only that, if you kill someone you really hate, that person will dominate your life even more, because you'll forever be vilified for killing them. Their memory will be inescapable, and it's all the worse for you if they're celebrated as a martyr. Whew—I'm soooo glad to get this off my chest! I've wanted to say it for a long time. If only I had the chance to tell the school shooters this, maybe they would have left their guns at home! Remember, it's far better to make a friend than an enemy. Or at least a passing acquaintance that doesn't make fun of you.

When boys call you ugly, they're actually saying they like you. It took me years to realize this. Some boys might come off like disgusting, worthless brutes, but that's all really just a disguise. In truth, they're too shy to admit how beautiful you are and how attracted they are to you! Spare yourself years of unnecessary pain and heartbreak by flashing the little stinkers a smile, and maybe even inviting them to your next birthday party!

Practice kissing your bare hand a lot. Just do this.

important!! →

Find a super-good place for your unsent love letters to various teen idols. And consider saving up to buy a sturdy lock box for them. Never, ever risk bringing them to school, either. I don't know if they still make Trapper Keepers, but if they do, I have news for you: In spite of the illusion of security they foster, Trapper Keepers do not trap written admissions of undying devotion to Patrick Swayze, Matt Dillon, Jack Wagner, or any of the Coreys. Nor do they keep them from being read over the school PA system on Senior Prank Day!

A Day in the Life of
Jean Teasdale

Ever wondered what I really do during my day? Is my routine anything but? Is it as wacky as one of my columns? Answer: Positively! Take a gander at my typical schedule.

6:00 a.m. Wake to alarm.

6:00 a.m. Hit snooze button.

6:10 a.m. Hit snooze button.

6:20 a.m. Hit snooze button.

6:30 a.m. Hit snooze button.

6:40 a.m. Hit snooze button.

6:50 a.m. Hit snooze button.

7:00 a.m. Hit snooze button.

7:10 a.m. Hit snooze button.

7:20 a.m. Hit snooze button.

7:30 a.m. Hit snooze button.

7:40 a.m. Hit snooze button.

7:50 a.m. Hit snooze button.

8:00 a.m. Hit snooze button.

8:10 a.m. Hit snooze button.

8:20 a.m. Hit snooze button.

8:30 a.m. Awake in panic, because I have to be at work at 9 a.m.!!

9:05 a.m. Arrive at work, punch in.

9:15 a.m. Get chewed out by supervisor for being five minutes late.

9:20–10:59 a.m. Sit around at cash register bored to tears because no customers have shown up.

11:00 a.m. When about to go on break, customer shows up at register!

11:10 a.m. Finally able to go on break.

11:11 a.m. Get my breakfast from vending machine (usually Drake's Cakes Devil Dogs and Dr. Pepper; Baked Lays and a Snapple if I'm on a health kick).

11:15 a.m. Glimpse a really fascinating article in *Good Housekeeping* (specifically, about a revolutionary new treatment for yeast infections).

11:30 a.m. Yelled at by supervisor to put down *Good Housekeeping* and get back to cash register!

11:30 a.m.–12:50 p.m. Sit around at cash register bored to tears because no customers have shown up.

12:51 p.m. Customer shows up.

1:00–1:34 p.m. When I'm about to go to lunch, customer finds some incorrectly marked-down clothing. She wants to buy it, but at the lower price. Since I got my customer override privilege taken away the last time I granted a discount, I follow company policy and tell her just because something is tagged wrong doesn't mean we accept the discount. "Discussion" ensues. "Discussion" ends when supervisor intervenes and gives her the discount anyway, making me look like a royal a-double-s!

1:35 p.m. Finally able to go to lunch, though I don't feel like eating.

1:40 p.m. Feeling a little hungry after all; go to Burger King across street, stand in long line.

1:55 p.m. My food is finally ready, but have only five minutes left in my lunch break!

2:00 p.m. Hustle back to work, unable to eat any of my lunch; supervisor gives me the evil eye for almost being late.

2:00–2:43 p.m. Sit around at cash register bored to tears because no customers have shown up. Suddenly, get a great idea! Want to jot it down in my notebook, but can't because supervisor doesn't let me write during working hours.

2:45 p.m.–2:51 p.m. Try to amuse self by picking out animal shapes on the frost patterns on the storefront windows and imagining them coming to life. It doesn't really work.

2:51 p.m. Customer shows up less than 10 minutes before the end of my shift.

2:59–3:20 p.m. Same customer comes to register to buy $70 worth of socks and a purse. Her Discover card is denied. She insists on going through her eight credit cards until the final one is accepted. It's annoying, but at the same time I totes relate.

3:25 p.m. Finally get to punch out.

3:40 p.m. Get home.

3:42 p.m. Nuke my Burger King meal (it never tastes as good as it does fresh—why is that?), settle down on couch, and watch my DVR'd soaps.

5:20 p.m. Decide to spend some quality time with my two kitties. However, as soon as they see Mommy Jean coming, they duck under the sofa.

5:30 p.m. Take a quick late-afternoon siesta.

10:00 p.m. Wake up in puddle of drool on sofa as a drunk Hubby Rick bursts loudly through the door with a take-out pizza.

10:00–10:20 p.m. Late dinner with Rick. He talks mostly in grunts.

10:45 p.m. As Rick passes out on carpet with an Xbox 360 controller and Priscilla the kitty perched on his tummy, I retire to our waterbed to finally write down

that great idea I had at work in my journal. Unfortunately, it has disappeared from my brain.

12:00 a.m. Fall asleep.

6:00 a.m. Wake to alarm.

6:00 a.m. Hit snooze button.

6:10 a.m. Hit snooze button.

6:20 a.m. Hit snooze button.

Health & Beauty Aid

I'm an absolute believer in the adage that beauty comes from the inside. After all, it works in my favor. Since there's a lot of me, that means I have more inside; ergo, my inside must be an absolute knockout! (Too bad there's no *Inside Beauty* magazine—I'd probably be its most famous cover girl!)

I've never been one of those gals to spend a lot of money on beauty gunk. For one thing, have you ever visited a makeup counter? Seventy-five bucks for a tiny jar of cold cream? Forty bucks for a tube of lipstick? No thanks, bub! I'd rather spend the money on things that will bring me real pleasure—a pretty doll, a mirrored keepsake box, a plastic chicken that poops out chocolate eggs—than something I'd just sweat off in an hour or two anyway.

Same goes with perfume. To me, Chanel, Prince Matchabelli, and all those snooty scents take a back seat to the most heavenly fragrance of all—brownies baking in the oven! And the smell of butter, sugar, and vanilla extract mixed together is a close second. I can't tell you how many times I started to bake sugar cookies, but never finished because I started sniffing the batter, then tasted it, and then— whoops, where did all the cookie dough go? (In fact, I'll go so far as to say that if a gal doesn't go around with a faint whiff of shortening about her, she is probably not to be trusted!)

To acquire that coveted inner beauty I mentioned earlier, first you have to think beautiful, gracious thoughts. I'm forever thinking about nice things, like how pretty wildflowers are, or my stuffed animal collection, or a tropical beach, or my favorite soap hunk-du-jour (Ryan on *All My Children*, anyone?), or the taste of chocolate! (Mmmmm!) Sometimes during stressful moments, like peak times at work or when I'm stalled in rush-hour traffic, I take long, languid flights of fancy, transforming my dull surroundings with such fabulous visions as floating down a barge on the Nile dressed in

linens and jewels like Cleopatra, all the while being fed grapes by Timothy Dalton and receiving a sesame oil rubdown from Kevin Sorbo! (Rowrrrr!)

Food has a lot to do with beauty, too. They say you are what you eat. If that's true, then today I'm a pumpkin cupcake, ten Hershey's Kisses, four large coffees with cream and sugar, half a bag of pretzels, an Orange Julius (I was at the mall), two slices of sausage and pepper pizza, and one Dove Bar! Doesn't sound so bad to me! I'm sugar and spice—literally! (Yes, I do have Type 2 diabetes. But I take medication to regulate it.)

Here's some other simple things us ladies can do to keep ourselves in the pink each and every day:

First of all, bathe or shower regularly. Once you do that, you're 85 percent there. Always be sure to wash between the folds, too. They're practically the most important! (I learned this vital necessity the hard way!)

Lotion obsessively. It's the only way to keep your skin baby soft! And don't forget those elbows! My favorite lotion is Rose Milk, but I also loooove Avon Skin-So-Soft. Not only does it keep your skin from flaking off in clumps, you smell like...well, you smell like lotion! (Also, if you've forgotten to wash your folds, it's a good way to mask the stench.)

I don't like to wear makeup very often, because it

feels so heavy and greasy on my face. I prefer to let my "natural glow" show through, anyway. However, I do love lip gloss. **To me, applying lip gloss is like treating your lips to a scrumptious fruit smoothie, but with none of the pesky calories!** My favorite kind is the flavored variety with sparklies in it. When I combine a sparkly peach lip gloss with my peach-colored sweats and my Rose Milk lotion, I feel like a luscious human sachet!

Beauty also means **keeping your body free and unconstricted.** I've never been one for tight-fitting clothing. To me, a defined waist is a confined waist! Buttons are for the birds—my personal rule is, if I can't pull it on over my head, then it's not worth the bother. That's why it will always be long, baggy T-shirts, sweatshirts, elastic-waist pants, and knit leggings for me—that is, unless Gymboree puts out a collection for adults!

As for hairstyles, I firmly believe that **the simplest ones are the nicest**—chuck those pesky curlers and straight irons in the trash! Take my hairdo, for example. I've had virtually the same one since middle school! Bottom line, you just can't go wrong with the classic Marcia Brady look. It's like growing two curtain panels off your head. What could be easier?

But I do acknowledge that change can be healthy.

I'll be the first one to agree that there's nothing wrong with a hair overhaul once in a while. Especially when you're going through some tough times in your life, or you're feeling a little down-in-the-dumps. For instance, about thirteen years ago, I was fired from a flower shop. I got home and was loosening my ponytail in front of the bathroom mirror (they always made me tie my hair back so my stray hairs wouldn't fall in the bouquets). I was having some trouble pulling the scrunchie out. Already feeling dejected and agitated, this pesky scrunchie was getting on my last nerve, so, before I knew it, I grabbed the kitchen shears and started giving myself a haircut. First, I whacked off the ponytail, then began chopping willy-nilly. Then I decided to refine it a little and go for a Winona Ryder pixie look. (It was the '90s, after all!)

I was doing dandy for a while, but then I cut a little too close in the back, the part I really couldn't see in the mirror, and I could feel a big bald spot. I tried to crop everything a little shorter, but that didn't work out too well, either. Suddenly, out of the corner of my eye, I spotted Hubby Rick's beard trimmer. I thought, why not? I clicked it to its most powerful setting and trimmed down the remaining hairs, and I trimmed them and I trimmed them, until, before I knew it, I became not so

much a Winona Jean but a Sinead O'Teasdale! Well, the stubble looked a little funny, so I put down Rick's trimmer, picked up his electric shaver, and took care of the rest! (I also shaved off my eyebrows, but I switched to a disposable razor for that.)

The whole thing was so much fun, I had a major case of the giggles! It was so freeing, too! I got so carried away that I decided to shave off everything else—my arms, my upper legs, and even my little thicket! (You know, where my pretty kitty lives!) The shaver would never be the same again—let's just say it bravely sacrificed itself in the line of fire! I skipped into the bedroom and twirled around and around in front of the closet mirror, relishing the feel of the cool air against my shaved head and everything else! (While doing this, I discovered that the space between my temples isn't as wide as my jaw. You sure notice interesting things about your head when it's hairless.)

Jean Proverb
#717

Don't let the realists get you down.

Well, once I was done, and the giggles subsided, stark terror shot through my hair-free body: Hubby Rick will absolutely kill me, I thought, and not just because

I killed his shaver and clogged his trimmer! Wouldn't you know it, the moment panic set in, Rick arrived! I hustled back into the bathroom and locked the door. Of course, Rick had to "take a leak," as he put it, but I refused to open up. Not even after he threatened to whiz in the kitchen sink. But what else could I do? I looked like the huge bald inmate from *Stir Crazy*! What was I thinking? Finally, after marshaling up every last inch of nerve, I told Rick that I did something pretty crazy, and I'd understand if he wouldn't want to have anything to do with me ever again. I wrapped a towel around me and opened the door, bracing myself for the biggest fight in our marriage since I got fired from the liquor store job.

adult Gymboree!!!

This could work!!

Rick's eyes were the widest I had ever seen them. They were the size of dimes. "What happened to all your

hair?" he asked. I told him, trying not to bawl. "Is all of it gone?" he asked. Yes, I said. "Everywhere?" he asked.

I dropped the towel.

Well, long story short, Rick didn't leave me. Wanna know what happened? For the first time in eons, he spent the night with me. And it wasn't no slumber party, Jeanketeers! Turns out that I, completely inadvertently, tapped into a little, previously unvoiced fantasy of Rick's. Who knew the hubby had a thing for completely hairless women? Certainly not me, and I'm his wife! Kinky, huh? Yeah, I thought it was a little weird, too. But considering the cold panic I had felt before, I wasn't about to question it. The next few days were pretty fun. But then I started to get these painful red shaving welts everywhere. Then things got incredibly itchy! I begged Rick not to touch me until my hair had grown back. (And he obliged me—even after my hair had returned!)

Going outside was a bit tricky, too. I made do with bandannas and baseball caps. But another unexpected thing happened: I actually got a lot of sympathy from strangers! At first I was puzzled, and it took me a while to make the connection: They thought I had cancer. And no, I didn't bother to correct them! It was nice getting some positive attention for once.

So my story shows that sometimes a change in your appearance can bring good things! And like the best things in life, you can do it practically for free!

Hair by Jean!

When your pal Jean does have hair, she likes to keep it simple! Ever wonder how I achieve my enviably effortless coiffure? Wonder no more!

First, I shampoo and condition my hair every other day. Bubble-gum scented shampoo is still my fave!

Once rinsed and out of the shower, I towel off my hair. While still damp, I part my hair and comb out the snarls. This is the only tough part. Yee-owch!

If I'm pressed for time, I blow-dry my wet hair. But when I have time, I let it air dry, passing the time with a fine magazine and a hot chocolate.

Brush a few strokes, and that's all you need to achieve the classic Jean-Do! Every few months, I take up my trusty scissors and trim the ends an inch or two. Or, if I'm feeling extravagant, I let the Supercuts ladies work their magic! What could be easier?

Alternate looks:

The "tuck behind the ear"

Ponytail!

Hubby Rick Is from Mars, Jean Is from Venus!

Golly, those differences between men and women truly are incredible, aren't they? Sometimes you would think we're two different species! Seriously, in a perfect world, wouldn't human women be married to kitties? Kind of like on that old TV series, *Beauty and the Beast*? (That show was soooo romantic by the way!) But think about it—women and kitties get along so well in general, and men and kitties stink up the bathroom and wreck household furniture at about the same rate anyhow, so why not? (Also, wouldn't a human baby-kitten hybrid be unimaginably adorable? That would be, like, cuteness doubled, literally! So get on the ball there, scientists!)

Hubby Rick and I are proof positive of the old adage that opposites attract, because boy, are we ever oppo-

Phew! Just thinking about this stuff makes me want to crack a window and get some air! Hubba hubba!!!

sites! (Actually, Rick may disagree that we "attract," but there you go, another area where we're opposite!)

Believe me, the differences between Hubby Rick and me could be their own book, and one almost as thick as the fall issue of *Redbook*! But I'll name just a choice few here. For instance, I know how to say when; Rick doesn't! If you asked Rick what "moderation" is, he'd probably tell you it's a part in a car engine! (Does this honk a horn, ladies?) For example, when Rick and I order delivery pizza, we can't just get one large pie—it has to be two. I'm content with four pieces, but Rick not only has to have the rest, but half of the second! Yep, we're talking one whole pizza for him alone! And sometimes there isn't even any of the second pie left over for the next morning's breakfast!

Don't even get me started about beer! Rick keeps a case of Coors on hand in the event of sudden dehydration, which apparently happens often to him, say every evening and all day Saturday and Sunday! Now, your pal Jean enjoys a nice, cool, refreshing alcoholic beverage once in a while—Brandy Alexanders, anyone?—but note the operative words "once in a while." Alcohol is more magical if you only have it occasionally. But try telling that to Hubby Rick! When Rick is on one of his drunks, sometimes I don't see him for the entire week-

end, sometimes longer if he takes time off work. He's either sleeping it off in the storage room of his favorite haunt, Tacky's Tavern (he has an in with Tacky, Jr.), in the bed of his pickup truck (he's had his wallet stolen twice and he still does it), or at the home of his buddy Craig (talk about another total piece of work!).

And Rick's the type of guy who considers his drinking a badge of honor. In fact, he ridicules me for getting tipsy on a single Long Island Iced Tea; he calls me a lightweight. He even has the nerve to blame his absences on me! He claims he would stay home more if I drank too, but instead, according to him, I'm about as fun to party with as a "comatose nun." Well, sorry to disappoint you, Rick, but getting drunk and having fun are not the same thing. And you know who agrees with me? No less an authority than Mothers Against Drunk Driving.

Here's the worst part, though: Even though Rick puts away twice the amount of pizza I do, and is Anheuser-Busch's biggest customer, for some reason he only outweighs me by ten pounds at the most. How in the name of Jenny Craig does that happen? (Sheesh, life is sure unfair sometimes!)

When it comes to animals, our differences aren't quite as stark. I love critters. Rick loves critters, too—

Easy — I work — Rick

dead ones! Question: Do other grown men like to shoot blackbirds with their dad's old .45 service revolver? I thought guys got over that stuff when they graduated from high school—not Rick. If a critter in our state can be legally hunted, you can believe Rick is up at the crack of dawn on the first day of its hunting season. He keeps his rifle at Craig's house; he started doing that after we got evicted from our previous apartment because he set it off while cleaning it and it shattered our glass porch door to thousands of pieces. (That wasn't the first time we got evicted because of Rick's hunting—we also got kicked out of Prairie View Residences because Rick would leave his kills in the basement, without bothering to field-dress them, and then, um, get drunk and forget about them. Ever gone downstairs to your apartment's laundry room and find an extremely deceased doe lying across the top loaders? Our building manager did!)

Rick doesn't limit his "love" for animals to hunting season, though. For a time, Rick fancied himself an animal control officer, and he bragged that he didn't even have to leave his truck to be one! I'd get very upset with him, but he'd explain that raccoons and squirrels were pests, always getting into garbage and building nests in chimneys, so he was doing society a favor. One night, Rick and I were driving home from a wedding,

and I saw a possum waddling across the lane. I covered my eyes, knowing what would happen next. Imagine my surprise when Rick actually drove around it! I commended him for turning a corner, but Rick told me the only reason why he didn't hit that possum with his pickup truck is because he was tired of hosing off the... aftermath...from his grille and underside of his engine. I should have known! Still, I suppose I should be happy he gave that possum a stay of execution.

All I can say is, thank goodness there's no open season on kitties—my Priscilla and Garfield would be forced into witness protection! Predictably, Rick can't stand kitties; he calls them the "fairies" of the animal world, and he's not talking about Tinkerbell! I adore my cats, and they mean the world to me. I'm always showering tons of attention on them, petting them, taking their photos, putting little doll dresses on them, you name it. I even give them people food! After all, cat food can get boring, so why not feed them stuff like cheese and ice cream and weisswurst? They snap it up like there's no tomorrow! Once I gave Garfield an entire roast beef and cheddar cheese sandwich for his birthday. He ate most of it, too, except for some of the bread, and the sun-dried tomatoes! (He threw up some of it later, but not all of it.)

So here's what I don't get. Clearly, to Rick's Elmer Fudd, I'm Elly May Clampett. But even though Rick hates kitties, Priscilla and Garfield seem to love him more! It's like the more he ig-

Jean Proverb #42

Is it possible to have a bad hair YEAR?

nores them, or refuses to make eye contact with them, or shoves them with the toe of his boot when they're in his way, the more they're attracted to him. They always want to sit on his lap, or rub against him, purr-ing like motorboats the entire time. It's like I'm not even alive! They never purr when I stroke them. In fact, sometimes Priscilla swats me with her paw, hisses, and races un-der the bed. (No matter, as I find kitties' diva-ish, take-no-prisoners attitude to be one of their most endearing traits!)

There's other habits Rick and I don't share, like gambling, watching soap operas, football, and bathing (I'll let you decide who likes what!). But probably the biggest difference between us is our scores on the old Love-O-Meter. I'm sure you love-starved wifeys can re-late to this one the most! I'm a woman, so I'm romantic

by nature. Our home is chock full of stuffed animals, lacy throw pillows, silk flowers, and vases. I always make sure there's clean, soft sheets on the bed, and floral air fresheners spewing their scented goodness from every electrical outlet. Granted, some of that is meant to distract from the litter-box smell. But I like to be surrounded by the things that remind me that life has its sunny side. And I'm a world-class cuddler, too. You guys out there who prefer your gals skinny are missing out on the sweet, fleshy warmth of a grade-A, plus-sized honey! Back when he was little, my cousin Mandy's boy told me that when I wore sweats, I felt just like a giant teddy bear! He used to hug me all the time, and try to lay his head between my...well, of course I never let him get that far, but you can see where it was going. (Our family was pretty shocked when we found out he turned out the way he did. I mean, we figured because he liked, well, those pillowy parts of the female anatomy that give milk...)

Unfortunately, I'm a cuddler who lacks a cuddlee. Yep, Hubby Rick is the type who doesn't like to be touched when he's trying to sleep. He says because he works his fanny off all day, he's entitled to some peaceful, undisturbed rest. Just my luck, huh? Now there's a guy who could stand to plug himself into some high-

DIFFERENCES BETWEEN MEN AND WOMEN!

Women talk in complete sentences;
men only communicate in grunts!

A woman's favorite room is the kitchen;
a man's is the bathroom!

Women remember anniversaries;
men only remember their own birthdays!

Men like beer; women would like beer if it
contained less alcohol and more chocolate!
(At least this woman would!)

Prior to whoopee, women love foreplay;
men think "foreplay" is some kind of golf term!

Women love the movie *Beaches*; men only love
movies of beaches that depict an Allied invasion or
show topless women!

Women agree to disagree; men disagree to disagree, because everyone should agree with them!

DIFFERENCES BETWEEN
MEN AND WOMEN!
CONT.

Once a month, women have their periods, and deal
with it; if men bled down there, they'd panic and
make a huge deal about it and probably call 911!

Women love cats; men love dogs (though, ironically,
they call women they think are ugly "dogs!" Which
brings me to my next observation: Women are
consistent, men are not!)

Men appreciate a home-cooked hot meal once in a
while; women just assumed the men were going to
bring pizza home again, and how is it all their fault?

Men don't come home for hours and hours, sometimes even days, and don't bother to call you to tell
you if they're okay; women call their men for every
little reason, like even if there's a squirrel at the
bird feeder, because they care about their men and
want to share every moment of their lives with them!

Women like to decorate their homes with things like
fragrant potpourri and floral throw pillows; men
will for no reason whatsoever suddenly shatter the
potpourri bowl against the wall and rip apart the
pillows with their teeth!

voltage hug power! Sometimes I think that if I could get Hubby Rick to cuddle with me more often, he'd be far less of a grouch. When I protest, though, he offers nothing but excuses. "I'd be more in the mood if you didn't have those creepy stuffed toys all over the place," Rick will say. "It don't turn me on to feel like I'm in a kid's bedroom. That's more Craig's thing." (Eeeek! T.M.I.! T.M.I.!)

Oh, it's not that Rick doesn't get frisky once in a while. It's just that, when he wants to make whoopee, it's the only thing he wants to do! I ask you, truthfully, what is so romantic about sex? I mean, it can be soooo uncomfortable...the sweat, and the slap-slap-slap noise, the low center of gravity, where to put your leg...the smells...and Rick makes these sounds...sort of like a badger clearing its throat...I'll mercifully spare you the rest!

So with Rick and me being practically from different planets, why, you may ask, do we stay together? Well, while I'm no mind reader, I think Rick sticks around because he's really just a softie at heart. He knows that his Wifey Jean keeps the home fires burning and assures him that, no matter what, she'll be there for him.

True story: Did you know Hubby Rick was the first-ever boy who kissed me? (Well, unless you count that

boy Dave in tenth grade, who did it on a dare from his teammates on the tennis team. But he laid his palm over my mouth and pressed his lips against the back of his hand to make it look like he was kissing me. And then he and the others had the nerve to call me "Slut-bag Jean" for the rest of the school year!)

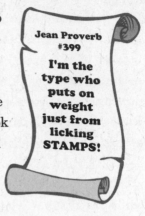

Jean Proverb #399

I'm the type who puts on weight just from licking STAMPS!

I remember the day as clear as glass—we were sitting in these woods just outside town, a place where the kids from my high school drank beer and generally engaged in monkey business. It was funny because, though I did have a bit of a crush on Rick, I wasn't thinking about kissing at all! As I recall, we were having a debate about the musical merits of one Rick Springfield, Dr. Noah Drake himself. Of course, as with every person of the masculine gender that he didn't like, Rick was questioning the manhood of the good doctor. He was of the opinion that the lyric, instead of going "I wish that I had Jessie's girl," was really supposed to be "I wish that I was Jessie's girl!" Rick was always saying stuff like that to press my buttons (what's new?).

So I said, wisecracker that I was in those days (what's new?), "Geez, Rick, with all your talk about 'gay' this and 'homo' that, one would think you had some kind of fixation on the subject!" Well, did Rick's face turn red! But do you know what he did next? Instead of saying something smart-alecky back, he took a quick look all around him, then, after realizing there was no one around to see, he pushed me down on my back, pinned my arms against the ground, and planted a huge wet one on my lips!

"A homo wouldn't do that, would he?" he said.

For a few seconds I was speechless. "Okay, you proved your point," I finally said. Then he kissed me again. I didn't know whether to struggle or yell for help. It certainly wasn't the loving, romantic first kiss I had always envisioned late at night in my bedroom. In fact, it was pretty sloppy—our family dog licked my nose with far more aplomb!

But then I remembered something my mother had told me just days before as we were shopping for clothes at Sears: "Being fussy isn't a right, Jean, it's a privilege. And you ain't earned it yet." I guess it was her "nice" way of saying "Beggars can't be choosers." So what can I say? I surrendered. But I drew the line at second base. (That was for another time—the next day!)

Don't you think that in these times of divorce and polygamy and non-commitment, it's pretty special that a woman married, and is still married to, her first and only kisser? Well, it warms my heart, at least. Besides, look at the alternative. Being single? No thanks, bub! That's just about as pathetic as you can get!

My Dream Wedding Dress!

Weddings—how romantic! (Le sigh!) For most of us ladies, it's the one and only time we are allowed to feel like princesses, only to become queens mere minutes later! Even though I got hitched back when Spandex leggings were all the rage the first time (!), I never ended my love affair with weddings. I still fantasize about my ideal wedding, and hold out hope that Hubby Rick will someday renew his vows to me in a gorgeous setting.

I suppose my deep desire to get married again stems from the fact that our original wedding left much to be desired, to say the least. It was thrown together quick as a wink, sorry to say. Because our

Where the dirty deed was done!

parents were all convinced that Rick would bolt to the state line in that Chevy Luv of his (which is where my mom and his dad found us making the whoopee that hastened the wedding in the first place), they made sure that we got hitched toot sweet! Had they actually let us take the time to plan a lovely affair, I probably wouldn't be renewing my *Brides* subscription for the nineteenth year in a row!

Where our parents were absolutely no help, however, was in footing the bill. That was all up to Rick and me, and we were not exactly rolling in the dinero! About the only positive thing I can say about the ceremony itself is that it mercifully clocked in at about 10 minutes, though even that seemed like an eternity.

Rick didn't even bother to shave, and galumphed to the altar wearing a tuxedo T-shirt at least two sizes too small for him! Boy, I'll never forget the look on Father Kelleher's face—Rick was lucky he wasn't excommunicated on the spot! As for me, well, I wish I could say I fared a lot better, but I didn't really. I was poorer than a church mouse on government cheese, and the wedding gowns I had tried on at the consignment and charity stores the weekend before were all too tight. So your blushing bride had no choice but to march down the aisle in a lime-green, circa-1980 prom dress "generously" donated by my stepsister Monica. Magical, huh?

The reception was held among a few picnic tables at Granite Grove State Park, just a stone's throw away from a dried-up lake bed where Rick burned old mattresses with his buddies for kicks. Our DJ was a tinny old boom box and a few cassette tapes! My mom didn't bother to attend the wedding. And she was the parent who was the most vocal about our becoming man and wife, though she was divorced (bitterly) from

Jean Proverb #114

Is Mrs. Dash the original Spice Girl?

my dad and couldn't stand the sight of Rick! Also, not five minutes after walking me down the aisle, my father ditched us to dine on steaks at his favorite supper club with Rick's dad.

It gets worse! I sat at a picnic table with Rick's senile grandmother, and, when she wasn't looking in my direction, I tried to sneak peeks at my teeny wedding ring that only fit my pinky. You see, the ring was the wedding band of this same grandmother; the family snuck it away from her when she wasn't looking. I tried my best to enjoy the funny-tasting double-decker Quinceanera cake. (At least it somewhat resembled a wedding cake. It was the fanciest thing the bakery had on hand at the last minute—otherwise they would have sold us a plain sheet cake.) Meanwhile, Rick and his boozy buddies engaged in—I kid you not—piggyback fights. You know, that game the rowdy boys played on the playground in sixth grade? Question: Do any of you longtime marrieds still dream about your old wedding and wake up in a cold sweat?

Later that night, in the "Afternoone Delighte" suite of the Romanticabins Motel, as I sipped sparkling cider, sat on a ceiling-mounted swing decorated with plastic flowers, and watched a blotto, pantsless Rick alternately whimper and snore on the heart-

Pineapple-flavored! (Yuck!) →

shaped bed, I made another vow that day: to never, ever, even when it seemed like life was hurling flaming cow-chips at me from every direction, lose my faith in true romance. This princess may not have felt much like a queen that day, but she would some day.

That's a major part of why, after much deep contemplation (and nearly breaking my imagination bone!), I've come up with an absolutely amazing wedding-dress design for myself. Admittedly, it will be a big expense, but the shoe box in which I've been squirreling away spare change (don't tell Rick!!) is starting to get hefty! And already I've found a person who has promised to create my dress for me: no, not Vera Wang, but my buddy Fulgencio! I met him a few years back while working in the data-entry department at SouthCentral Insurance, and boy is he a supportive friend! When I first described the dress to him, he let out a shriek and said, "Girl, if you actually manage to put the cash together to buy the materials, I will slave day and night

Fulgencio!

making it free of charge. Just shackle me to the sewing machine and whip my [tushie] if I start to nod off!" You see, besides being a complete peach, Fulgencio is a

gifted costume designer—he makes gowns for whom I like to call his "dress-up friends." And get this—these dress-up friends are guys who like to wear women's clothes!! Ah, well, to each his own! (Personally, I can't fault a guy who wants to look like a girl, since I look like a girl, too. I call it having good taste!)

My dream wedding dress has a lot of details, but these are the most important:

1. First, it would be made of only the richest silks, satins, and lace of snow-white so blinding, you would have to wear ski goggles to look at it! No in-between shades like cream or ivory, and certainly no lime-green!

2. The skirt is wide and billowing and supported by a hoopskirt underneath. I love hoopskirts because they swoosh around so gracefully, and immediately remind me of Scarlett O'Hara and *Gone with the Wind*, the very apex of romance!. Plus its fullness will make my waistline look small in contrast! Not only that, if I have to go to the bathroom, I can just lift up the skirt and turn it inside out as I seat myself in the stall. (See, I've thought of everything!)

3. Big, puffy sleeves! Sleeves need to return to wedding gowns. They look like shapeless toothpaste tubes these days. Bring back the opulence!

4. Swarovski crystals and seed pearls everywhere you rest your eyes! (Hmmm...wonder if you can load a Bedazzler with precious gems?)

5. A cake frosting–inspired sash around the middle of the skirt, gathered with bows accentuated with diamonds! (The goal is to not only resemble Scarlett O'Hara, but a beautiful wedding cake and a capitol building, too!)

6. A lace veil secured with a priceless diamond tiara. I don't necessarily expect to own the tiara, so I figure the local Jared can lend me one, just like Harry Winston loans jewels to the stars for the Oscars.

7. A 20-foot train, decorated with my initials and ideally carried down the aisle by at least half a dozen multicultural children.

8. As for shoes? You're probably thinking sky-high Jimmy Choos or fairy-tale glass slippers, right? Wrong!

fancy
lace veil
(tablecloth-
quality)

beautiful glasses!
(crystals)

20 ft. train
(held by small
multi-cultural
children!)

my
grandmother's
antique pearl
necklace (let out)

beautiful
sweetheart
brooch!!

exquisite beadwork!

hoop skirt
(figure-flattering!!)

pink high-tops! (surprise!!)

by Jean!
(with drawing
help from
Fulgencio!)

Pink high tops! Surprise!! I thought I'd throw in a little fun to bring all the dazzling glamour a bit down to earth. I'm a regular gal at heart, after all. Besides, I've rarely worn high heels, and I don't want to trip and fall into the eight-foot-tall wedding cake I've planned, too!

Phew! I get dizzy even thinking about this incredible work of art! Traipsing down the aisle in that show-stoppin' jaw-dropper, I figure it won't really matter what Hubby Rick wears. If he wants to put on the shredded remnants of his old tuxedo T-shirt that he keeps in a sack of oily rags in his pickup truck, he can go right ahead! Heck, maybe I'll just renew my wedding vows all by myself! Because I will be walking, breathing proof that true romance still lives…and thrives!

Things About Jean
that Bug the Shit Out of Me,
by Hubby Rick

CANT HOLD DOWN A JOB

HER CATS

KEEPS A FUCKING BUNNY-TISSUE-COVER-THING
IN BATHROOM

STINKS OF LOTION

ALWAYS TAKING MY BASEBALL CAPS
& PUTTING THEM IN CLOSET

STANDS IN FRONT OF TV WHEN
I'M WATCHING IT

LEAVES LONG BROWN HAIRS
IN MY TRUCK

SINGS

~~THE~~ HOGS COVERS

ALWAYS ~~HER~~ HAS GOOEY SPARKELY
SHIT ON HER LIPS

KEEPS NAGING ME TO BUY
RASBERRY BEER

SIGNS HER NAME WITH A SMILY FACE

MOLES ON CHEST

KEEPS BUYING SHIT
SHE DONT ~~REALY~~ NEED

HER CHICK FLIX MIXED
UP WITH MY VIDEO GAMES

WONT LET ME SMOKE WEED,
LIKE SHES MY MOM OR
SOMETHING

BRETH STINKS OF SOUR
CHOCLATE

ALWAYS SEWING AND KNITING
SHIT BUT NEVER FINISHS

YELLOW TEETH

MUGS HAVE TO BE PUT IN
CABINETT WITH HANDELS
STICKING OUT TOWARDS YOU

TAPES DUMB HAERTS TO
APARTMENT WINDOWS
FOR ♥ VALANTINES DAY

WANTS TO CELABRATE
VALANTINES DAY

ONLY BUYS SOAP THAT SMELLS LIKE
GIRL PERFUME

COLECTS FRIDGE MAGNETS

LEAVES HER GIANT BRAS OUT

BITCHES WHEN-I SCALE
FISH IN LIVING ROOM

HER LAUGH

ALWAYS BAKING SOME WIERD
CHOCLATE THING

FUSSY CRAP ON OUR WALLS, FAKE FLOWERS EVERYWHERE

PICKS UP PENNYS ON SIDEWALK & ALWAYS HAS TO SAY "LUCKY PENNY LUCKY PENNY" OUT LOUD

FREAKS OUT WHENEVER SHE FINDS A BARLEY LEGAL IN MY DOWN VEST

HAS BIG TITS ONLY BECAUSE SHES BIG EVERYWHERE ELSE

Lovin' from Jean's Oven

No. 2:
Ooey Gooey Choco-Cocoa-Mocha Cupcakes with Raspberry Filling and Coconut-Cream-Cheese-Cola Frosting!

Another in-Jean-ious recipe that will have you wondering how such wildly varied ingredients can add up to one absolutely droolicious cuppycake recipe! Of course, you won't wonder for long—in seconds you'll lapse into a helpless cocoa-coma!

For cupcakes:
1⅔ cups flour
¼ tsp. salt

½ tsp. baking powder

¼ cup unsweetened cocoa

2 squares unsweetened chocolate

4 tbsp. butter

⅔ cup light brown sugar, packed

2 eggs

1 tsp. vanilla

⅓ cup whole milk

½ cup strong black coffee, cooled to room temperature
(That's where the "mocha" comes in! Genius, huh?)

For raspberry filling:

1 10 oz. package frozen raspberries, or 1½ cups fresh
raspberries

¼ cup water

¼ cup granulated sugar

2 tbsp. cornstarch

1 tsp. lemon juice

For frosting:

8 oz. cream cheese

½ cup (1 stick) butter

6 tbsp. cola (Again, your eyes don't deceive—cola! And
no diet cola allowed! Jean Teasdale never cuts cor-
ners—or calories!)

2 tsp. vanilla
3½ cups confectioners' sugar
1 cup flaked coconut

First, preheat your oven to 350° F, whip out your handy-dandy 12-cup muffin pan, and line the cups with paper cupcake liners. (Preferably decorated with cute kitties or bunnies!)

Second, prepare your raspberry filling. Combine all the ingredients in a saucepan and stir over low heat until the filling comes to a boil and thickens. Remove saucepan from heat and chill in the fridge while you prepare the cupcake batter.

Now, sift the flour, salt, baking powder, and cocoa into a bowl and stir until blended. In another saucepan, melt the squares of unsweetened chocolate, butter, and brown sugar over low heat, giving it a good stir. Once it's all melted through, remove the saucepan from the heat. Pour the mixture into another bowl, then add the two eggs and beat gently. Now pour in the vanilla, milk, and coffee, and stir until combined. Add a little bit of the liquid mixture to the dry ingredients, stopping to stir it all together. Pour in a little more liquid mixture, and stir again. Keep doing this until you run out of liquid mixture and everything is combined.

It's nearly time for your oven to make happy little cuppycake friends! But before you do anything else, retrieve the raspberry filling you've already prepared from the fridge. Here's the real fun part—time to load up that muffin pan. Spoon enough batter into a cup until you're just short of the halfway mark. Then add one spoonful of the raspberry filling into the center of the batter. Cover the filling with one or two more spoonfuls of batter, until the cup is three-quarters full. Keep doing that for each cup. When you're done, pop the cupcakes in the oven and bake for 30–35 minutes.

As your cupcakes bake, work on the frosting. Beat the cream cheese and butter together until it's one big delectable pale yellow mass. (I know it's hard, but please, resist the urge to devour it!) Add the cola and vanilla and mix. Now pour half a cup of the confection-

Sometimes I bake only in an apron !!

ers' sugar into the sifter, and sift into the frosting batter. Stir until the confectioners' sugar is completely combined. Repeat this step for each remaining half-cup of confectioners' sugar until all of it is combined. Donezo!

When your cupcakes are baked, remove them from the muffin pan and let them cool for an hour or so. After frosting each cupcake, sprinkle the top with coconut. And you now have 12 amazing Ooey Gooey Choco-Cocoa-Mocha Cupcakes with Raspberry Filling and Coconut-Cream-Cheese-Cola Frosting. Inhale!

Sheesh, Writing a Book Is Hard!

Is it bad that I'm not even halfway through this book and already straining for topics? Believe me, I'm as surprised as you are, especially considering the massive amount of time I've put into this puppy! But I'm coming to the rather disturbing realization that maybe all my preexisting wit and wisdom, so lovingly recorded in my trusty Lisa Frank notebook, might not fill an average-sized book. I don't understand it. I really thought I had enough material. Why wouldn't I? It always seems like I'm scribbling something down. After all, I'm rarely without my notebook and something to write with, usually a six-color pen. And yes, I use all the colors, even the hard-to-make-out orange! (I just had another horrid thought—what if I'm unwittingly repeating myself and forcing my readers to re-read words I've already written?)

I hope I can come up with more things to discuss. But after chocolate, cats, shopping, and hubbies who can be real stubby, I ask you, what else is there to talk about? What else is there to relate to?

I have to keep soldiering on. I have to commit to this thing. After all, it's probably too late for me to do a complete 180 and, like, write in the character of an ax murderer, right? Maybe a few of you wouldn't mind, but it simply wouldn't be convincing. It would leave too many loose threads. Plus I think I'm way too beloved among my Jeanketeers to inexplicably change into an evil person, even if it would be strictly fictional.

Perhaps I shouldn't be telling you this, especially since you've read this far already, but sometimes I get these sneaking thoughts that I shouldn't be writing this book. That it doesn't have a solid reason to exist. That the premise is too thin. That no one cares about my recipes, or how I maintain my hairstyle, or what color my part-time parachute is. Or what if I'm not digging deep enough? I thought I was pouring my heart out on these pages, but what if I'm not being truly honest with myself? They're dark, sinister thoughts, I know, and defeating and counterproductive ones, too. But I can't help but wonder if they're right. Then I start to worry if these are the types of thoughts people

get shortly before they have a nervous breakdown or do something desperate. Did Erma Bombeck ever suffer nervous breakdowns? Did she ever dangle her kids from penthouse ledges? Oh, of course not. I'm sure she had her act together. Unlike me. This is just stuff out of my brain—it isn't supposed to be hard work! So why does it feel like it?

Oh, snap out of it, Jeannie! Don't be such a Fretful Francie! Try to see the big picture. People just want me to entertain them and make them laugh. Yes, I must keep that in mind. Fear not, Jeanketeers. I may have hit a little snag, but I'll get my mojo back. (Maybe, if I'm lucky, Erma Bombeck's ghost will visit me one night and give me some great ideas. That would be kind of scary, admittedly, but also very helpful.)

What Is a Friend?

A *friend is someone who shows up with a triple-layer mocha-coconut-fudge cake with cherry filling and says, "It's your birthday"—even when it isn't!*

A friend has your back...and front, and sides, and hopefully waist size, too! (So you can share clothes!)

A friend is familiar with everything you do. You could quiz a friend on the most intimate details of your life, from who your first crush was to what section of the banana bread you consider the tastiest.*

If she cannot answer these questions, then she is not a good friend.

* The crusty corner

A friend understands and accepts your need to make ghosts out of Kleenex, even when it isn't Halloween.

A friend's love is unconditional (and on hot summer days when your electricity has shorted out, air conditional!).

A friend will come over to your apartment at 3 a.m. and stun a bat with a broom for you. Then, because you feel upset and guilty about it, at dawn she and you will stage a funeral for it in the vacant lot near your apartment building.

A friend lets you cry on her shoulder. (She doesn't even mind if you absentmindedly wipe a visible streak of snot across it, too!)

Catsitting? Not a problem with a real friend.

A friend never stares at you for a good long minute, then asks, "Have you ever considered waxing your upper lip?"

"Or your sideburns?"

"Or your nostrils?"

Your friend would be proud, nay, honored, to wear your face on a T-shirt, if necessity dictates.

A friend can also have four paws. (Preferably de-clawed!)

Or a friend can have buttons for eyes.

A hot-water bottle can be an amazing friend.

Some of the greatest friends can be ones you've never met face-to-face. I am speaking, of course, of friends on daytime television. Among my greatest pals through the years: Rosie O'Donnell, Oprah Winfrey, Hoda Kotb, the Snuggle Bear, the lady announcer who read the Community Calendar on WMBL-TV in the mid-1980s, Gary Collins, and Nancy from Sewing with Nancy.

A friend, I hope, is you!

But if you don't consider me a friend back, that's okay too.

(P.S. In case you don't consider me a friend back, I hope there is at least one special friend in your life who meets all or most of the above criteria. And if there isn't, find one! Your new friend could be as close as the nearest Build-A-Bear Workshop or your TV screen!)

(P.P.S. Um, why don't you consider me a friend?)

My First Column from (Gulp) 1990!

Jean's Note: As I mentioned before, my association with The Onion *newspaper stretches back two decades! It all started on that lazy summer day in 1990 when, having recently graduated from high school and dating not-quite-Hubby Rick, something told me to enter the annual "Fill the Third-to-the-Back Page of* The Onion" *contest. And guess who had the winning entry? Yep, it was the first (and so far only) thing I'd ever won, too! I used my $50 grand prize to—no lie—buy my very first Precious Moments figurine!*

As if I wasn't already elated enough, days later, a call came from Onion *Women's Preoccupations Editor LeeRae Boggs asking me for more columns! (She said I captured the voice of "confused girls transitioning to womanhood" well.) The columns later developed into the*

"A Room of Jean's Own" feature we know and love today. The rest, as they say, is history! (Well, no one really says that, at least not to my face. But this inaugural column is pretty historic to me!)

the ONION

AUGUST 28, 1990

Day 24 In Deely Boppers and Counting!

By Jean Speidr

If you've been around and about our humble little burg, chances are you've seen a pleasantly plump, bespectacled young woman bopping down the street. Nothing special in that, I suppose...until you realize this same young woman is literally bopping—in a pair of deely boppers!!

I confess, my fellow citizens—I'm that deely boppers gal. Allow me to introduce myself—my name is Jean Speidr, Grissom High Class of '89 (Go Orbits! Blast off to State!), and I've just completed my 24th straight day wearing these rad little bouncy antennae!

Yes, you read right! For over three weeks, these crazy things haven't left my cabeza except when I wash my hair. I even sleep with them at night—I simply secure the sides with hair tape and put cotton balls between the top section and my head so it doesn't chafe, and presto! Slumber has never been more wonderfully wacky!

What inspired me to take my fashion cues from space aliens and insects? Well, it's simple. Anyone who knows me knows that my life is all about spreading a little joy and whimsy to others! I'm sure I've brightened many a day with my funny little

stunt! Also, they help me cope with the terrible shock I received after finding out that ultra-hunk of my dreams Patrick Swayze is married.

I mean, when did this happen? I had no idea. I had never heard that Patrick Swayze had a wife. And I read *People* religiously! How could I have possibly missed this? And apparently he's been married for, like, 15 years. Fifteen years? 1975? That's sooooo long ago! (Like, when he was busy tying the knot, I was probably in my bedroom giving my Crissy doll a haircut!)

So you can imagine how crushed I was when I caught this interview on *Entertainment Tonight* with Patrick Swayze, looking as yummalicious as ever, with this sleek-looking blonde lady. I bet she would never be caught dead in deely boppers (though I suppose a woman of her age shouldn't be wearing them anyway! Hmmph!). Patrick Swayze and this lady looked all happy and cozy together. I bawled like a baby! Then I promptly medicated with a pint of chocolate Häagen-Dazs. But this die-hard choco-lover only felt bloated—and no less blue! Why, Patrick Swayze,

why? (In case you didn't notice, I like to refer to him by his entire name. That way I get to write it again and again! Patrick Swayze Patrick Swayze Patrick Swayze Patrick Swayze!)

It's true that Patrick Swayze and I come from different walks of life. He's a studly Texas hoofer, and I get winded climbing the stairs in my mom's house (where I still live). He's a red-hot superstar, and thanks to a recently changed law (thanks, state legislature!), I'm not even old enough to drink. (Except for the occasional Brandy Alexander—don't tell my mom!) But I still liked to think that I had a chance, however teeny. Also, I loved making my main squeeze, Boytoy Rick, jealous! Rick knows all about my thing for Mr. Swayze and it eats him up! He disapproves of male dancers, and always calls Patrick Swayze "Patrick Gayze." Sheesh! Too bad Patrick Swayze doesn't bottle and sell his classiness, because Rick could sure use some. Isn't it obvious that deep down, the boytoy is green with envy? (Sometimes I think I should give this Rick Teasdale the old heave-ho. But then I remember how much fun it is to have him

wrapped around my finger!)

As I said, I felt down in the dumps about Patrick Swayze's marital status. But then I thought, hey: There's plenty of other hot young celebrity fish in the sea! There's always C. Thomas Howell, and I hear this Richard Grieco guy scores high on the hunkitude. And, of course, not only Milli, but Vanilli! (I think I'll pass on those "grunge" rockers, though—ewww!)

Then I arrived at an even bigger thought: I've got my entire life ahead of me. Why concede defeat of any kind now? I'm only one year out of high school and more or less unattached (the boy-toy and me aren't that serious). I'm starting a new job next week at Heinie's Bowl-It working at its shoe and concession booth (gee, wonder if they'll let me wear my deely-boppers?), and I'm considering vocational school next year. But I have no concrete long-term plans, nor do I want any right now. The way I see it, I have loads of time to both acquire options and weigh them!

So Patrick Swayze is hitched. Whoop-dee-doo! I've got at least a good 10, possibly 15 years of other hunk obsessions (Fabio, anyone?) ahead of me! Once this all dawned on me, out went the negative thoughts, and on went the deely boppers!

So here's to a bright future—a future so bright, I gotta wear deely boppers!

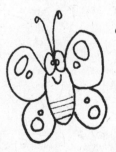

Boy, wasn't junior Jean a real space cadet? I totally forgot about that deely boppers escapade. (They didn't let me wear them at Heinie's Bowl-It.) And to be honest, though I never really recovered from my disappointment over Patrick Swayze's marital status, I kept fantasizing about him anyway—couldn't help it!

Plus I never went to vocational school, and I got married to Hubby Rick within weeks ("Boytoy Rick" sounds

a little clumsy to the ear anyway!). And check out that rambling prose! Wow, I did tend to go on a bit, didn't I? I've become a much better self-editor. Still, irresistible little time capsules like these serve to remind yourself where you came from, and how far you've gone!

My Most Memorable
False-Alarm Pregnancies!

May 1986

Might as well start off with my very first one! I was a high school sophomore, and Auntie Flo (tee-hee!) hadn't paid a visit for two months. I also noticed that my jeans were getting tighter and tighter around the waist. I began to fret. True, I hadn't been with a boy yet. (Back then, I was preserving my virtue for the blond Simon of *Simon & Simon*! RrrROWL!) But being Catholic, I wondered if some divine intervention had occurred! I never knowingly experienced an angel visiting me or a sunbeam lighting up my tummy, but just to be on the safe side and get into character, I'd recite the rosary and walk around my bedroom with a white bed sheet safety-pinned under my chin and a paper plate taped to the top of my head.

Well, one day, without warning, my mom barged into my room with her laundry basket, and saw me and went ballistic because she thought I was making fun of religion. That forced me to have to explain my situation, and of course, my mom, being my mom, automatically feared the worse ("You're so gullible, you'd do what any boy would tell you to, and shame me in the process!" she yelled—whatta cutup she is!). She immediately hauled me off to the urgent-care clinic. Long story short, the pregnancy test that my mom insisted on came up negative (of course), and boy, was the overworked doctor not happy to discover that I was still a virgo intacta (that's fancy-talk for "nothing's been fiddled with down there!!")! He grumbled that carrying a few extra pounds sometimes made you, uh, gush less often down there. And just my luck—the very next day, the red menace (tee-hee again!) arrived. If it had only arrived twenty-four hours earlier, I would have been spared a lot of embarrassment! Oh well, it was so long ago that we can all laugh about it now!

October 1995

Okay, okay, I admit this one is pretty dumb! By this time, I had been married to Hubby Rick for a few years, but we were still known to make some pretty rough

waves on the waterbed on occasion (hot-cha-cha)! One morning I decided to try out one of those home pregnancy tests, you know, the wand-like thing you make a wish and wee-wee on? So I almost turned a cartwheel when my pregnancy test read positive! At home that evening, I decided to surprise Rick by placing the wand among his take-out french fries when he wasn't looking. He bit into it and nearly cracked a tooth! Naturally that freaked him out a tad, but before he could sue Hardee's, I told him that I had stuck it in there. After about half-a-minute or so of cursing, Mr. Sophisticated asked me what the h-e-double-hockey-sticks this thing was. "Silly!" I replied. "This told me this morning that a little Jean is on the way!"

I never saw Rick move so fast as he did driving me to the twenty-four-hour drugstore and making me buy a new test. (He was sweating like the Bridal Veil Falls was tumbling over him, and even more remarkable, he didn't even bother to finish his Hardee's!) He was up at the crack of dawn and practically dragged me out of bed and sat me on the toilet. Once again it read positive. "I don't see anything," Rick said. "You sure?" "Of course," I said. "No line means preggers!" I got kind of annoyed when Rick immediately started fishing through the trash for the box the test came in—boy, he's a support,

isn't he?

Well, turns out Rick's skepticism was valid after all. See, I thought no line on the display meant positive— you know, a line usually means minus, or negative, right? Guess I should have read the instructions more carefully. Guess I should have read the instructions!

Thankfully, these days they've come up with some pretty goof-proof pregnancy tests—they all but hit you on the head with the result! I haven't made this mistake ever since. That second test also marked the first and so far last time I've seen Rick cry. Well, cry and giggle with joy at the same time.

May 1998

I was glowing—radiant even! People at work noticed it, too. They remarked on how rosy and unblemished my skin was. Some even asked if I stopped putting five tablespoons of coffee in my sugar every morning (no typo!). Yet I hadn't changed a thing about my diet. Instead, I just felt really good that month—spring was in full, fragrant force, the lilacs were blooming, the robins were out doing their robin stuff, and, oh, I don't know, I just felt like I shared in their joy, too, like I was a small but essential part of the world, too. I started to think about ducks hatching ducklings, bunnies having baby

bunnies, and honeybees dividing into baby honeybees, or however baby honeybees are made. I'm very much in touch with my feelings, and it dawned on me that maybe all these warm sentiments were telling me that something wonderful was going on inside me too. It was a totally blissed-out feeling, one I've only experienced a couple times in my life. Also, when I feel this way, I shop.

And boy, did I shop! To the tune of $1,896.72! That was the combined price of the nursery furniture, the baby clothes and accessories, and the sales tax and delivery costs of same! Yeah, this time I was so sure that, before taking a pregnancy test or going to the doctor or anything, I whipped out the plastic and splurged the splurge of my life! I tried to buy sale items when I could, but I just couldn't resist that full-price lace christening gown, that darling Disney Babies crib mobile, or a lamp that plays music as it projects stars on the wall, or a doorway swing with pink plush cushions. (My feelings were also telling me the baby was a girl!) I was dizzy with excitement. I couldn't believe that I, too, was buy-

Jean Proverb #31

Don't worry about painting yourself into a corner, as long as you choose a nice color!

ing and owning the same things I've seen people with babies flaunt! If there's anything that comes closest to a Teasdalian heroin rush, it was signing that purchase receipt for the changing table. I lost all concept of space and time, not to mention budget!

It didn't take Hubby Rick too long to figure out the credit card had been maxed out (he was rejected for a routine purchase of Slim Jims and WD-40). But before he could scream at me upon entering our apartment, the words were knocked right out of his mouth by all the cardboard boxes and plastic shopping bags taking up the living room! Instead, he just stared at me with an expression that I'd never seen on him before, and it didn't change for a long time, not even as I triumphantly explained my condition to him and how it was so important to get a head-start in readying for a baby. Rick said nothing, then uttered quietly, "I think you should turn around and use the john, Jean." I was puzzled, then followed his eyeballs down to the place they had settled. As I emerged from the bathroom freshly tampooned and my stained sweatpants soaking in the sink, I noticed that Rick's face had slackened and turned gray. I'm not sure if it changed any more colors, as it was pretty hard to look him in the face afterwards.

Not one of my red-letter days! (Pun not of intended!)

No doubt, I should have thought before I bought. Certainly, had I known the only thing that would pop out of my oven was a blood pudding, I wouldn't have embarked on my little escapade! Fortunately, most items were returnable, though it was an awful hassle hoisting them back into the car and calling stores to cancel deliveries for the stuff that hadn't arrived yet. But I don't think you Jeanketeers will hold it against me too much that I held on to a few baby clothes and toys. (They're still in a cardboard box marked "Someday...")

February 2000

This was the time I had pseudocyesis! It's a rare medical condition; the most famous example was some English queen who reigned thousands of years ago. Pseudocyesis is a fancy term for "your body is a pregnancy prankster!" My belly swelled up, my joints hurt, I suffered morning sickness, the works! Sure, I was pretty blue when I found out my symptoms were all false. But what mostly made up for it was all the attention I received! My physician, Dr. Plimm, was pretty amazed. He had previously assumed pseudocyesis was a mythical disorder. He actually took me to a nearby medical college to have some people there examine me.

I think he invited some interns from the hospital to sit in, too. (Even the doctor guy who hosted the "Cheers to Your Health!" segment on *TV News 12* was there! Though he didn't bring a camera crew, which to this day I have mixed feelings about.) I even got to go to Minneapolis for a couple days to be poked and prodded by a couple specialists. I stayed at a nice hotel and everything! I also own a couple copies of the medical journal I was featured in, though I've never been able to get through the article—after all, I'm no Alberta Einstein!

I always wanted to be associated with something rare, or better yet, do something completely unique, but I was thinking more along the lines of finding a treasure chest or being able to fly! We're all special, it's true, but I hope this wasn't my only crack at being super-special!

March 2004

My period was more of a question mark, and I had been having dizziness and numbness spells for several weeks. Which only meant one thing: Road trip to Gymboree! Well, after conferring with a store clerk, who had previously only known me as a wistful browser, on a newborn layette and getting on a baby-shower regis-

try, I did something rather unusual for me—I passed out. One emergency-room visit and hasty appointment with Dr. Plimm later, I discovered my symptoms were due to—get ready—Type 2 diabetes! Boy, was my face red! (And my wee-wee sugary!)

In the years since, I've become a pretty good blood-checker and insulin-injector, but I still haven't produced a Mini-Me pitter-pattering her little feet about Casa Teasdale. My biological clock is still ticking (though often it seems like it's flashing "12:00 a.m." in red LCD letters!). All I can say is, keep watching that clock, Jeanketeers!

Things
I Have Burned,
by Hubby Rick

HALF AN ABANDONED TRALER

DUMPSTER *

COUCH
(AT GRANETE
GROVE STATE PARK)

ANTS

SHITLOAD OF
HOT WEELS CARS

FREINDS PENTHOUSES
(SETLING A SCORE)

ARMY MEN

DISCO RECORDS

SACK OF JIGSAW PUZLES
I FOUND AT GOODWILL
DROP OFF. YOU CAN FIND
SHIT TO BURN THERE

BALSA WOOD AIRPLANES
SOKED IN GLUE

MATRESS
(AT GRANETE GROVE
STATE ● PARK)

HONDA SPREE SCOOTER
PARKED OUTSIDE
SOME CAMPUS BULDING.
IT WAS IN 1986. COME GET ME FUZ

PICNIC TABEL (G.G.S.P.)

BOX OF COMBS

COTTON WOOL

ESTES ROCKET
(DIDNT GO OFF SO WE JUST
SET IT ON FIRE)

ONCE BURNED MY HAIR
LIGTING JOINT IN WIND.
FREIND PUT IT OUT.
DONT REMEMBER MUCH.
GOT NICE MULLET OUT OF
IT THOUGH

TYPEWRITER

A KITCHEN ✳

CHILDRENS SLEEPWEAR

CDS (I REALLY BURNED THEM. WITH A ⊗ PROPANE TORCH)

ALMOST BURNED A PLYMOUTH SWINGER. LONG FUCKING STORY WITH THAT

ONE OF JEANS STUFED ANIMALS. TORCHED IT OVER A STOVE BURNER WHEN SHE WAS OUT SHOPING. HEH HEH

＊ DIDNT MEAN TO

Part 2: If I Was Elected President (Hey, It Could Happen!)

The U.S. Capitol, Washington, D.C.
January 2021

My fellow Americans,

First of all, let me warmly thank you for entrusting me with the highest office in the land. Believe me when I say that, as the first female president of the United States, I do not take my mandate to govern lightly. And by electing me to the White House with more than 90 percent of the popular vote, you have told me in no uncertain terms that change must come, and I will do my utmost to bring it. I intend to exercise my political capital to the fullest, for the benefit of all Americans.

(Huge applause)

First of all, I hereby declare by executive order that all Americans, regardless of color, creed, gender, or age, are required to have fun at least four hours every weekday, and six hours on Saturday and Sunday. Whether it's flying kites, pulling taffy, or rearranging your stuffed animal collection, fun activities should not be considered a privilege for a few, but a right for all!

(Huge applause)

All workaholics found to be violating this order will face a hefty monetary fine, or must administer mandatory foot-rubs to random fun-havers chosen in a lottery based on Social Security numbers.

(Applause)

Secondly, all fit people must put on a minimum of 15 pounds. You've made the rest of us feel inadequate and uncomfortable long enough.

(Huge applause)

Thirdly, I will establish a program that will bring inexpensive and delicious chocolate to the sugar-de-

prived in the poor and war-torn nations of the Third World. Isn't it about time these unfortunates got a sweet-treat break?

(Cheers of agreement, applause)

There is more. My vice-president, beloved talk-show host and media mogul Oprah Winfrey, known more popularly as "Oprah," will also serve on my Cabinet as Esteem Czar, a move I'm sure will delight every human being in the United States.

(Cheers, chants of "Oprah! Oprah! Oprah!")

All world leaders who promote warfare and genocide will be rounded up by our armed forces and finally put in a small room where they can fight it out. This has been discussed for countless generations, but I'm finally making it a reality!

(Deafening applause)

I'm not done yet, my fellow Americans. I will also authorize funds to construct a memorial in Washington, D.C., consecrated to those who have devoted and even sacrificed their lives to furthering the cause of cuteness.

(Applause)

Inspired by the example of the nation's new First Man, Hubby Rick...

(Applause mixed with boos)

...all qualifying American males will be enrolled in a mandatory remedial romance course, so that they may finally acquire valuable and lasting skills in pleasing—and pleasuring—their mates!

(Cheers mixed with gasps, oohs, ahhs, and nervous giggles)

Every two months, the wonderful mommies of our great land, who are the very bedrock of society, will get a Saturday off solely to relax and indulge themselves, while all childless American women between the ages

of fourteen to seventy will babysit their children! And if these childless women are anything like me, they're absolutely thrilled to undertake such a great privilege and noble task! After all, who doesn't loooove kids?

(Roars of approval)

Jean Proverb
#608

Double
the
chins,
double
the fun!

Now, I know that there are some of you, a small minority but an assertive one nonetheless, who are critical of my policies. Some of you do not enjoy cute things. Some of you feel that a 15-pound weight gain could pose health hazards to some. Some of you believe that the government should not play a role in the romantic rehabilitation of errant hubbies.

(Some booing and hissing)

Now, now. I know that the overwhelming majority of you reject this ideology. But this is a time for malice towards none and charity for all. Let me say that while I cannot admit I completely understand

♡ **163** ♡

the opposing positions, I respect the feelings of those who espouse them, and I reach out my hand in warm friendship. I hope to work closely with leaders of the opposition, and to reassure them that their misgivings will fade during my term. We have much to learn from each other, but I believe an open mind and a judicious belief in compromise can only benefit our nation in the long term. This will be the driving and overarching point in the mass reeducation retreats my administration will be opening throughout the country, so that skeptics may grow to understand and appreciate my policies and viewpoint. All of this will become clearer as time passes.

(Applause)

Now, I know tradition dictates that inaugural addresses be lengthy, but it's going to be a long day, what with the parade and the balls and everything, and we want to squeeze as much fun as we can into every minute. Therefore, I will close by saying that if you want to find out more about my positions, go to www. jeanteasdaleswhitehousefun.org. I will be updating the site every time I get a new idea, so be sure to visit it often.

(Applause)

My fellow Americans, the next four years are going to be a challenge, but they're also going to be the best this country's ever had. You believed in me enough to elect me to this great office, now permit me to carry out the immense work that lies before me. My office hours, by the way, are 9 a.m. to 3 p.m. Monday through Friday, Saturday from noon to 3 p.m., and Sunday I'm closed, but I do check email. God bless each and every one of you, and God bless the United States of America!

(Deafening applause, shouts of "Jean! Jean! Jean!")

Lovin' from Jean's Oven

No. 3:
Jean's "In Your Face, Diabetes!!" Choco-Wallow!

I may have Type 2 diabetes, but it sure doesn't have me! As proof, I offer this scrumptious no-bake concoction that will make you feel like you're mired in a chocolate-filled ditch with no hopes of ever climbing out (yummm)! I try to bake it whenever possible. After all, this is what they make insulin for, am I right?

Ingredients:

2 boxes instant chocolate pudding

3 cups chocolate-flavored whole milk

9 oz. non-dairy whipped topping

2 tbsp. chocolate syrup

About one box (approx. 14 oz.) graham crackers (chocolate-flavored graham crackers or wafers even better!)

For the frosting:

3 packets pre-melted unsweetened chocolate, or four blocks of unsweetened chocolate

3 tsp. corn syrup

2 tsp. vanilla extract

3 tbsp. butter or margarine, softened

3 tbsp. chocolate-flavored whole milk

1⅔ cups confectioners' sugar

19.2 oz. bag M&M's plain candies (optional, but why hold back?)

In a bowl, combine the two boxes of instant pudding with the chocolate milk and lovingly transform them into chocolate pudding. This takes a few minutes even with an electric mixer, so feel free to watch your favorite TV shows as you do this! Once the pudding is firm, measure out the whipped topping, add the chocolate syrup to it, mix, then fold the whipped topping into the pudding mixture until completely blended.

Now it's time to make the frosting. (If you are using blocks of unsweetened chocolate, first melt them in

a double boiler.) In a separate bowl, combine all ingredients, except the M&M's, and mix. Easy!

Take out a 9 x 13-inch pan. Cover the bottom with
one layer of graham crackers. Then spread a layer of
the pudding-whipped topping mixture atop them. Top
that with another layer of graham crackers. Spread
another layer of pudding-whipped topping mixture.
Get the picture? Keep doing it until you come just
short of the rim of the pan. Then frost that topmost
layer, and dot it with as many M&M's as you please.
Cover the pan tightly and chill in your fridge for at
least twenty-four hours.

*Now, it's very likely you'll be left with some extra
frosting. That's on purpose—it's my gift to you for having to wait twenty-four agonizing hours to enjoy a slice
of this mocha chocolata ya ya! So treat your tongue to
all those batter- and frosting-covered bowls, spoons, and
mixing blades (the latter preferably detached from the
mixer)! There, not so lifestyle-altering now, eh, Type 2
diabetes?*

*(Seriously, don't eat the Choco-Wallow before the
twenty-fourhours are up. The graham crackers have to
break down and get mushy first. I know from firsthand
experience!)*

It Takes All Kinds!

Ever notice all the people in the world? They're everywhere! Not only that, they all have their own personalities. Even my own small corner of the globe is chock-a-block with some real characters! Human diversity is part of what makes life rich and interesting, and the people in my neighborhood don't disappoint! Yet for all their unique quirks, I think you'd be pretty hard-pressed not to find at least a couple of them verrrry familiar—heck, you might even be one of them! All I can say is, if you've gone through life and have never encountered one of these kinds of people, I have to wonder just what the rock you've been living under is made of! (J.K.!!!!!)

Kids Who Mock You in Traffic!

So, as you're happily putt-putt-putting along in your merry automobile, a station wagon passes you and pulls in front of you. In the rear is a gang of 11- and 12-year-boys fresh from soccer practice. But instead of talking among themselves or bothering the driver like normal kids, they've decided to shower their attention on little old you! They're making odd faces and some extremely naughty hand gestures—and while you can't know it for sure, you're pretty certain that one of them mouthed the words "Do me fat mama." Maybe they were influenced by all that "M.I.L.M.W.T." ("Mother I'd Like to Make Whoopee To"—I refuse to be vulgar) stuff on TV, but whatever it is, it makes you wish that whoever was driving would go through a car wash with the windows down, so those kids could get their mouths cleaned out with soap!

The Old Man Who Winks at You!

This friendly fellow sure can add some unexpected sunshine to your day! He comes in many different forms: He's the guy who stands in front of the neighborhood tavern; the guy who mows the lawn of your apartment building; the guy who checks off your name at the polling place; the guy driving the Lincoln Town

Car; the guy buying foot cream at the Pamida; the guy awaiting his early-bird special at Ruby Tuesday's; or even the guy sitting in the women's department waiting for his wife to try on clothes. You're not completely sure why you're a frequent receiver of old-guy winks, but you like to think it's because you're doing something right! Maybe you remind him of someone he once knew, or maybe he's just seeing if his old lady-killer chops still work. Whatever, it's very sweet and cute! (That is, until he unzips his pants and shows you what's underneath. Which has happened a couple times.)

Whoever Drops Off Those Shopper Flyers on Your Front Step!

Who is this mysterious person? Is it a kid looking to make some extra money? A retired person looking to make some extra money? Beats the heck out of me. I've waited outside for hours on my balcony and for some reason I can't seem to catch him or her in the act. If I go inside for even a few seconds to get a juice or something, I emerge to find a bunch of them on the step. And they'll show up any time of day; it's never consistent. Maybe we're not meant to know who this person (?) is. Sort of

like the unknown soul who takes the coins out of the basement washers and dryers every couple weeks. (I gave up on that one years ago.)

The Bossy Supervisor!

Where do they find these people, anyhow? In mean camps? Everybody's had one: If you so much as place your chin in your hand for two seconds she asks you how your work is coming along, or if you would like some more work to do. She keeps an eye on you every time you make a personal phone call. She periodically reminds you of the office dress code, even though only a stone-cold grump would disapprove of someone wearing a pretty pair of strawberry-colored leggings with a beaded panda sweatshirt! And then she promotes the girl who graduated from high school only a few months ago, even though you have tons more work experience and are far friendlier and would have had an incentive to make fewer mistakes if you had gotten the promotion! Sheesh! (Give the Bossy Supervisor 50,000 cc's of chocolate, stat!)

The Friend Who Never Calls!

Guess she's just busy! Oh well!

The Medical Clinic Receptionist!

The Medical Clinic Receptionist is quite a character—actually, she would be at home among some of the Batman villains! She smiles about as often as Mt. Rushmore, cancels your appointment when you're ten minutes late due to traffic, or makes you fill out a *Thorn Birds*–sized form, even if you already filled it out the last time you were at the doctor's! She even gives you a dirty look when you innocently help yourself to a lollipop from the receptionist station—"Those really are for the children, you know."

The Stuck-Up Clothing Store Clerk!

The Stuck-Up Clothing Store Clerk is the cousin of the Medical Clinic Receptionist! She thinks you'll shoplift every last nylon knee-high at Dressbarn if she doesn't keep her leery eyes on you every second. Or worse, she clearly doesn't think you're good enough to be shopping at her store. Even the gal at Catherine's Stout Shoppe has been known to roll an eye or two at your presence! Sheesh again! Maybe you look too much like a fish-out-of-water, particularly if you're not a big clothing shopper. But once in a while, when you're forced to try on actual pants, it would be nice if someone could fetch you some larger sizes as you need

them. That way you won't have to leave the fitting room and hobble to the middle of the store in too-tight pants which end up having to be cut off you anyway, and in the process get stuck with a bill for $45.37!

The Waitress Who Waits On You Last!

The Waitress Who Waits On You Last is the best friend of both the Medical Clinic Receptionist and the Stuck-Up Clothing Store Clerk! She's the one who takes your order after the previous table, even though they got seated ten minutes after you. Then it just so happens that the entree you order is the one that takes the kitchen the longest to prepare—or so she claims. Of course, despite her rudeness, the hubby's busy making eyes at her, and chalks up your disapproval of her service to mere jealousy! Can you believe that? Well, despite all that, you tip her generously, because you remember the days you yourself worked as a waitress, plus you don't want to rile her up even more. But you're definitely never coming back to that restaurant again. (Well, at least when she's working there.)

Your Best Friend in High School!

We all had one, and we all remember her fondly. She was the girl who let you eat with her at lunch; who

picked you for her volleyball team in gym class, sparing you the humiliation of being picked last by picking you next-to-last; who once gave you a clay bookmark she made in ceramics class; who let you have her used Nikes; and even invited you to her birthday party!

Years later, at a class reunion at your school, you spotted her right away. As you talked to her, it seemed like no time had passed. It was wonderful; you somehow felt you had come home. Well, at least until she asked you who you were. Totally understandable—you had absentmindedly stuck your nametag in your purse rather than wearing it. Even after you put it on, it took her a couple minutes to realize that you and she were best friends once. You talked for a few more minutes, and she excused herself to use the bathroom. You didn't see her for nearly two hours. Then you finally came across her in the football field bleachers as she drank and smoked with a bunch of people with whom you had never socialized. She was having so much fun laughing it up with them that you decided it was best to leave her be and cherish your memories. She was really a great gal.

Ya know, now that I read through this, maybe I really don't know a lot of different types of people after

all. I was going to talk about the Snobby Postal Worker, but then I realized it would be another retread of the Medical Clinic Receptionist, except in a different workplace of course. Guess I should get out more. Or maybe a lot of cranky and narrow-minded jerks happen to live in my town. But on the bright side, perhaps, much like a gorgeous tapestry, cranky and narrow-minded jerks come in all sorts of different colors and textures!

Jean Salutes Mommies!

Of all the people I observe in my daily life, I'd have to say the one who has it made the most is the Mommy. After all, Mommies have the most important job in the world, and the most fun one, too! Can you imagine being surrounded all day by adorable kids who love you, and even better, adorable kids who love you and who popped out of your own personal uterus? Well, maybe you can, because you could already be living it! If there are any Mommies who still feel underappreciated these days, well, they haven't met Jean Teasdale. For they have my instant and undying respect, gratitude, and, might I add, purplest, purplest envy! (Do you see the drool coming out of my mouth?)

A Mommy commands powers the rest of us don't— besides being able to give life, which is soooo amazingly

incredible, it seems like everything she says and does
has, well, a natural air of authority and superiority to
it. My poor words can't do it justice, but I've witnessed
it firsthand, and it is a wonder to behold. For example,
a Mommy can, without asking, enter the middle of a
long line with her kids, and no one will object. In fact,
the folks in line are often happy to lose a place or two.
They'd never tolerate that with a single person, even
if that person had to pee real badly. And why should
they—after all, where are that person's kids? At the
many jobs I've held through the years, common was the
refrain "Sue will be late again this morning" or "Pat
will be in at 9:45." And it was perfectly fine, because
they were Mommies! Obviously, they had some problems getting the children off to school, or the washing
machine broke because someone overloaded it with too
many dirty clothes, or baby got his tiny hand stuck in
the baby gate. We didn't think twice about it. Because
we'd have to be total ogres to expect a Mommy—who
birthed us into this world, after all—to be at work on
time along with the childless people. My gosh, even baby-
spit-stained T-shirts look like ermine robes on them!

If I'm working at some job in which I interact with
customers, I find it a true privilege to receive a snide remark from a Mommy. Once upon a time, I used to think

it was the overreaction of an overwhelmed, stressed-out parent, but that was the selfish way of looking at it. The truth is, I, with my cold and empty baby oven, am simply not her social equal. Only another Mommy can judge a Mommy, and even that depends on how many children she has relative to the Mommy she's judging, and whether any of them are adopted.

Just imagine if I was a Mommy. I would be treated with complete respect. If I pushed my child in a stroller, I'd never have to open a door myself. No one would ever second-guess me again. I wouldn't get weird looks at Gymboree any more. People would smile at me.

The Mommy, in short, is the empress of the universe. How I sorely wish I were one. Maybe someday, God willing.

Bartender, Pour Me a Nice, Tall Glass of Shopahol!

If, by chance, you were at the mall this weekend, and a small tornado made of plastic bags whizzed past you in the parking lot, that was no weather phenomenon: Instead, you unwittingly observed your ol' pal Jean on a shopping run!

There are three constants in my life: Hubby Rick, yeast infections (eww but true), and buying things! Even in my most broke and jobless state, I've always reserved some disposable income for fun stuff! Although it depends on what you define as "disposable." As Hubby Rick so sweetly puts it, "The only way any of our income is disposable is if you throw it straight in the trash, which you practically do anyhow!" (See, he never made these types of jokes before he married me—shows how my sense of humor has rubbed off on him!)

Yep, just call me Jean the hopeless shopaholic! My chronic shopaholism has no easy cure, but the nice part is, I don't want to be cured! It has brought me oodles of joy and fills in that empty feeling I sometimes get (I call it "the empties"). I don't know if anyone in my neck of the woods requires the services of a personal impulse shopper, but if there is, they should contact me lickety-split. I have a lot of free time (or when I don't, I can make it), and I work cheap! If you don't believe in my shopping prowess, you need only stick your nose in my shopping bags. This is—I kid you not!—a list of items I bought in just one weekend:

Precious Moments "Take It on the Lamb" figurine—The Precious Moments folks do it again! I'm an avid P.M. collector, and my latest acquisition is an unbelievably megacute figurine of two boy and girl moppets bandaging a lamb. Not sure if they're bandaging the lamb because they're playing doctor, or if the lamb is actually injured. Whichever, it's utterly adorable (I assume the lamb represents Jesus). The best $50 I spent this week!

Eight scented candles—Did you know that Jean Teasdale is the original aromatherapist? It's true— since I inhaled deeply from my first room air freshener as a small child, I knew that lovely odors could have

a direct and positive effect on your mood! I've always loved floral fragrances, but in the last few years I've graduated to more unconventional scents like fresh rainwater and baking gingerbread. Guess it's all about becoming more sophisticated! The biggest treat about scented candles is lighting them all at once and letting their fragrances waft and mingle. In minutes, my home smells like an apple cinnamon lavender lilac violet orange blossom sandalwood sea breeze! (They also make for a great Hubby Rick repellent!)

Campbell's Soup Kids salt and pepper shakers—Just another set for my collection! Acquiring salt and pepper shakers is a longtime hobby of mine, too. I'm no shrink, but I think it's my way of coping with my debilitating pepper allergy. It's true—if I come into contact with pepper, I start sneezing like crazy! (Gotcha! Had you for a second there, didn't I?)

Sillier String—Saw this at the Park 'N Pik and I just had to find out exactly why this string was sillier than the classic original! The answer: Every few feet, the string suddenly comes out in a humungous clot, and as it does it makes a very rude noise! It's like the can is sick or something. Okay, it was a waste of money, and afterwards I spent a long time cleaning up all the gunk in the living room, but I must admit, it suckered

me, and you don't discover anything new unless you take risks!

Ballerina hippo top with glitter—Okay, get your defibrillator ready for this one, because you're in for a huge shock: There is one thing I hate shopping for—clothes! I'm about as eager to try on a pair of jeans as I am about contracting mad cow disease! (Yuck!) But if there's one item of clothing I can't resist, it's a top with cute things embroidered on it. A lavender-colored cotton pullover top with a ballerina hippo design appeals to that little Garanimals wearer that still lives inside me. (Like Peter Pan and Michael Jackson, I've never grown up!) What's more, it was only $8.99 at the Pamida, marked down from $13.99! It's so nice, I think I will reserve it only for special occasions in which I must dress to impress. A job interview, for example.

"Baby's First Christmas" ornament—Okay, okay, it's not Christmas, and it's not baby's first. In fact, there's no baby. But this was an absolute can't-resist must-have! A darling little ceramic baby sleeping on a glitter-covered Star of Bethlehem? Would I pass that one over? Please, what am I, dead?

Interesting foreign snack food—Dollar General is my commanding officer! I can't resist stopping in there at least once a week to see what new stock

it has. Lately I've been enjoying this chicken-flavored noodle-looking stuff in its food section. I don't know what it's called, because the package is printed in Oriental. Hubby Rick refuses to try any of it, because he thinks that any food made by Orientals, even fried rice, is made up of "at least one-quarter cat"! Hoo-boy, how narrow-minded can you get? At least there's one adventurous person in the family!

Anyhow, get this—besides being all in an unreadable language, the noodle snack's package is decorated with a black child in a grass skirt and a bone through his nose. I don't get the connection. I would think the mascot would be a child with slitty eyes and a triangle hat. Maybe it is indeed a misprint, which would explain why they're at Dollar General. Ah well (or should I say "Ah so"?). The snacks satisfy my hankering for the savory, but I wish the Oriental candies at Dollar General could quench my craving for the sweet. So far I've only sampled these little chewy waxy things with a cute white bunny on the package. But the white bunny is the only thing in their favor (and flavor!). It's made me reluctant to try the other sweets there. I suppose that's where my adventurousness ends; if this is the Oriental version of sweet, what if everything else tastes like fish or soy sauce?

"Greetings Pussy" soap dispenser—
Another Dollar General find! Some genius in
one of those Oriental countries (again!) came
up with an affordable alternative to Hello
Kitty for the budget-minded cute connois-
seur (namely yours truly!). Thoughtful! Only
sometimes the English on these items is a little
strange—I have a clipboard decorated with a
cute frog playing soccer, and underneath him
reads the inscription "Always endeavor mag-
isterially for triumph." I don't think English
speakers usually talk that way. Except maybe
in England.

**Corn holders shaped like smaller pieces
of corn**—Yet another Dollar General gem! You
can't have enough of these things! Especially
when sometimes the yellow plastic parts get
eaten along with the real corn. (I confess, both
the hubby and I are guilty.)

Kitty Dizzier—Look what the Jean
dragged in—yep, yet another kitty toy! In fact,
Casa Teasdale wouldn't be Casa Teasdale without a living room two inches deep in kitty toys!
My latest acquisition is the "Kitty Dizzier,"
which is jingle-bells, tinsel, and a cute little cro-

cheted snake tied to a plastic rod. It may not sound impressive, but the clerk at the pet supply store said her own kitty went nuts for it, so what can I say? I had to have my Priscilla and Garfield test it out. Well, so far, Prissy has lived up to her name and simply walked into the bedroom after I wiggled it at her. Garfield, however, hasn't left its side since I brought it home! No, he hasn't chased after it—instead, he plopped down beside it and licked the snake. And he's still at it! Okay, so Garfield's a little—how shall I say—unique. I think it comes out of the same side of him that tries to mate with the bath rug. But it's part of what makes our feline friends so very endearing, right?

Girl tools—I still can't believe what a find this was. Whoever conceived this idea is a genius! They took regular hand tools like pliers, wrenches, screwdrivers, hex keys, a hammer, a tape measure, etc., and decorated their handles with a pretty floral pattern, then encased them all in a pink tool box! Voilà—at long last, tools for us without Y chromosomes, and they're no longer in embarrassing and ugly colors like black and gray! Move over big boys—guess you're not the only act in town anymore!

I couldn't wait to show Hubby Rick that I now had my very own tools. At first he didn't get it, saying that

we already had a tool kit. When I opened the case, he laughed and said they were garbage and he had much better tools in his truck. I should have known he'd say something like that! Rick always tries to take the air out your sails when you have something over him. Then he said, "I bet you paid like fifty bucks for them, didn't you?" Nooooo, smarty pants! Try $46.99! And they were on sale! So who's the tool now, Rick?

I can't wait until we have a plumbing or radiator problem, so I can put all my girl tools in action and show Rick what real girl power is! (Well, except for the hammer. As I was testing it against the kitchen table, the hammerhead flew off and put a dent in the drywall.)

A frog-with-a-fishing-pole figurine you hang off the edge of your computer monitor—Self-explanatory, but a real day-brightener! One of those silly things that keep my spirits up! My only criticism of it so far is that the little string hanging off his pole obscures the screen a smidge. It creates a bit of a distraction as I write. No problem though, it just keeps me on my toes!

A humdinger of a list, am I right? And I'm not even counting necessities like cotton balls, milk, light bulbs, and beer! As for holiday shopping, forget it! You don't

want to even be near me! All I can say is, don't reach for something too close to me at the clearance jewelry table at T.J.Maxx—you might draw back a bloody stump! Just kidding!! I am not really a violent person. But I do like shopping for the holidays.

The Needle's Approaching Empty, Jeanketeers

Is it too late for you Jeanketeers to form a prayer circle for me? I think I'll need some divine intervention to finish this book. Then again, if you're reading this, it most likely means that I did finish the book, and it got published. But the Jean of the present doesn't know this. All she knows is, she has sixty pages left, and no earthly idea how to fill them.

I must confess something rather embarrassing. I rarely finish anything I set out to accomplish. Jobs, craft projects, you name it. It's like I never have closure. I work at a job for a couple months and then I get my pink slip. No satisfying exit, no "moving on to better things," not even a lousy going-away party with Hawaiian Punch and stale cupcakes from the supermarket! And my hallway closet is spilling over with empty oatmeal boxes. Oatmeal boxes that are loudly

crying out at me to become piggy banks with push-pin legs! Wonderful, but when, Jean, when?

Speaking of crafts, right now I'm staring at a hook rug of a frog that is draped over the rattan chair in my bedroom. I began it around Easter of last year. It's only one-quarter finished. I only hooked the top part of the yellow background and his white eyes. A pair of huge, white, unblinking eyes, staring at me, never breaking their gaze. Eyes that follow me as I walk around the room. Mocking eyes!

I know it must seem strange that a veteran newspaper columnist is having problems finishing her own book. You're probably wondering why I just can't apply the same discipline I use in my column-writing. The truth is, I'm good at words—I'm just not used to writing a thousand of them every day! Have you ever tried it? Well, if you haven't, don't judge!

I find it a little suspicious that no one from the beginning of this project has offered to help me. Don't authors often use ghostwriters? I remember reading that one of my all-time favorite romance-novel authors had someone else write her last ten books for her. At the time, I felt crushed, and even cheated. But now I fully comprehend the beautiful and perfect sense of it. Writing sucks up soooo much of your precious time. When

you factor in all the time you spend merely thinking about what to write, you practically get an eternity! You can spend hours at your kitchen table (or, as I prefer to call mine, breakfast nook) in front of a ream of Wind Song–scented stationery and barely eke out a single sentence. While all this is happening, or not happening, life is passing you by! The sun is shining, a refreshing breeze teasingly blows your curtains, and you're missing all kinds of great daytime TV!

I just put the frog rug in a drawer. But I can still feel his eyes.

No one told me anything about hiring a ghostwriter. I will have to take that up with the publisher. It doesn't seem professional not to at least offer the option. If I had to do it over, I definitely would've hired a Jeanketeer to write at least half of this book. Oh, you Jeanketeers know my voice. Just talk about chocolate and cats, then rhymes-with-witch about Hubby Rick and you're there! Okay, bitch! Bitch! I said it! I just swore! BITCH! Here's another one—damn! DAMNATION TO HELL!

Sorry. Just having one of those days! I really don't know what else to add. I guess that's what they mean by writer's block. If anything, this proves beyond a doubt that I didn't use a ghostwriter, because if I had, you wouldn't be reading any of this!

Jean's Trivial Purr-suit!

1. What is my favorite household chore?

a) Vacuuming

b) Laundry

c) Dishes

d) Wiping down the mini-blinds

The answer is, natch, d, wiping down the mini-blinds! Can't tell you why, but I get a lot of pleasure out of cleaning the grime off each blade with a paper towel dipped in a solution of Mr. Clean and water. I mean, a lot of pleasure. Sometimes I clean my mini-blinds three times a week. I probably have the cleanest ones in town! (My cats' litter box, however, is a different story!) All I can say is, if cleaning your mini-blinds several times a week is wrong, then I don't want to be right!

2. The following cartoon character does NOT adorn any piece from my prize jelly jar collection:
a) Foghorn Leghorn
b) Mario
c) Smurfs
d) Muppets

The answer is b, Mario! Never really cottoned to any of those video game characters, maybe because Hubby Rick played (plays) video games so much! You know, as I look over my dozens of jelly jars, it strikes me that I've eaten an enormous amount of grape jelly through the years. It makes me feel a bit nauseous. I should get my mind off it! Think of kittens! Think of kittens! (Oh, now I'm thinking of kitten jelly, which is even worse!!)

3. What are the names of the children I one day hope to have?
a) Rhett, Schuyler, and Antoinette
b) Tyler, Taylor, and Tai
c) Quentin, Holden, and Courtney
d) Arrowsmith, Scout, and Fonzie Lou

If you answered letter b, you were warm—those are

the names of my brother Kevin's kids. Answer c is way off, though—I absolutely despise the name Quentin. It's almost as bad as Mitchell. Instead, the answer is a, Rhett, Schuyler, and Antoinette! They're the perfect combination of romance, historical reference, and pure class. Plus I can call the girl a coveted "i" name—Toni! (See "The Name Game" to get what I mean). However, give yourself partial credit if you answered choice d. Those are the names I would consider if I became super-famous, like Angelina Jolie famous.

4. What was my hair color as a child?
a) Dark brown
b) Black
c) I did not have hair

You seriously thought I didn't have hair as a child? Puh-lease! I wasn't a freak! The answer is a, dark brown. (It's my hair color as an adult as well, proving that yes, brunettes do have more fun!)

5. At what age did I start wearing glasses?
a) 5
b) 11
c) 19

The answer is b, 11. I didn't really need them, but my mom somehow talked our family optometrist into corrective lenses for me because she argued my eyesight would get worse anyway and it would teach me humility as I entered my "awkward years." While my mom was technically right about my eyes getting worse, to this day I'm not really sure how she managed to convince a professional eye doctor to prescribe thick glasses to a girl with 20-20 eyesight. Then again, my mom's powers of persuasion have always been very strong.

6. What was I arrested for back in 2000?
a) Choking Hubby Rick
b) Shoplifting circus peanuts from the Pamida
c) Breaking into a school

Answer a only belongs in the realm of fantasy, folks! And I would never, ever do c. That is just wrong. It was my brother Kevin who broke into the school. He tried to steal big cans of rubber cement and turpentine from the art room and got caught by the night janitor. As I mentioned earlier, he had a side business selling trucker stimulants, and he thought he would get into the gluehead market, too. (Kevin has really turned his

life around and is practically a different person. He's a born-again Christian now!) No, I shoplifted the circus peanuts. It was a rough time. I had just lost a job and I was feeling kind of lost. But worry not—I'm fully rehabilitated now. I will never steal circus peanuts again, cross my heart!

7. What was my worst job ever?

a) Data entry at SouthCentral Insurance
b) Picking up trash along Highway DX
c) Giving out restaurant flyers in a cow costume

This is a little bit of a trick question, I'm afraid! If you answered b, you would be wrong. True, it was a terrible job, but it wasn't technically a job for pay. It was actually my community service punishment for shoplifting from the Pamida. C is incorrect as well. Wearing a cow costume and passing out flyers? If only! Sadly, I've never been one of the lucky chosen. I saw a person doing it the other day for a new steakhouse that just opened, and I bet you could spot the green on my face for blocks around. The answer is a, data entry at SouthCentral Insurance. That job was a real soul-killer, as I previously noted. I got a lot of flak for my lack of keyboard skills (their opinion, not mine!), but I

eventually got fired from it for using the internet during work hours. Turns out losing that job was a blessing! It eventually led to my stint at Fashion Bug. Okay,
maybe it wasn't so much a blessing, because I lost the
Fashion Bug job, too.

8. In a 1995 column, "Daydreaming for Fun (If Not Profit!!)" I described a new color. What was it?
a) Blacknge
b) Pinklow
c) Broud

The answer is c, broud! It's the color of the inside
of your eyelids when you shut your eyes tight and push
the ball of your hand up against your closed eyes. Seriously, it's a very unusual color, and one I've never seen
depicted anywhere or overheard mentioned. It's sort of
like a burgundy-green, but that description falls far
short. Strangely, the people in charge of colors have
never contacted me about it. (Who are they, by the
way?) Also, the color broud smells like nutmeg. I kid
you not!

SCORES

If you got 7-8 questions right...

You know so much about me I should take out
a restraining order against you! J.K.!!!!

If you got 5-6 questions right...

Not bad, but your Jeanketeer status is a bit shaky.

If you got 3-4 questions right...

You need to bone up on your Jean studies.

If you got 0-2 questions right...

I can't help but feel a little hurt.

Jean's Letters to God, Book II

Dear God,

   If there is indeed alien life on other planets, do You love them as much as You do us? Even if they're all green or look like giant insects and lay eggs in hosts' chests and that sort of thing? Really?

Love,

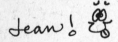 Jean!

....

Dear God,

   Why did You pick Roman times to send Your only Son to us to redeem our sins? I ask just because it was such a long time ago, and most people today aren't very interested in ancient history. To them, anything longer

than fifty years ago is practically caveman days. Why didn't You send Him now, when life is so much more complicated? Plus, overall it would have been safer for Your son. We don't have crucifixion anymore, and people today are inclined to be smarter and nicer and are into self-help and spiritual stuff. Jesus could have been on TV. Then we could just have the coming of the Antichrist and Armageddon and all that stuff later. I'm not saying You were wrong—You're God, after all, and You call the shots—but I'm just wondering why the Roman times to send down Jesus.

Love anyhow,

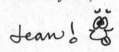

Jean!

....

Dear God,

Remember that Raggedy Ann sweatshirt I used to wear in high school? Well, one day when I was sixteen, it disappeared. You must remember this: It went missing from my locker after third period gym class, and the gym teacher gave me a holey (not holy, I mean it had holes), worn-out boy's T-shirt for me to wear around for the rest of the day, and the fabric was so thin you could see my bra underneath! I tried to get

my Mom to pick me up from class early, but she said no because I needed my education, so everyone saw my predicament and made fun of me. Well, that's all water under the bridge now. But I loved that sweatshirt and I've long yearned to find out what happened to it. I will accept whatever fate it met, I just want to know.
Love,

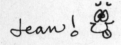

....

Dear God,

I just wanted to thank You for the glorious sunset You blessed us with today. It looked just like one of those photos you see of a tropical beach, even though it was just in my neighborhood. It made me feel good.
Love,

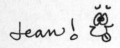

....

Dear God,

I am writing You to pray for peace in the world and the end of all wars. I never wrote this before because I thought it was an obvious thing to say, but then I real-

ized You might not think I care about that stuff. I didn't want there to be a misunderstanding on Your end.

Love,

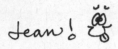

....

Dear God,

I was watching a science show about the solar system for a few minutes today, and started wondering if Jupiter is Hell. It looks like a very nasty place, filled with poisonous gases and constant storms. And if it is Hell, is Hitler there? Hope these questions aren't too much of a bummer.

Love,

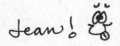

....

Dear God,

If I'm doing anything that will increase my chances of going to Hell, please let me know. So far I think I'm a-okay, but maybe there's something I'm doing wrong that I'm not aware of. Sometimes You put voices in people's heads—can You put one in mine? Not a crazy one

that makes me kill people, but one that gives me use-
ful, common sense advice.
Love,

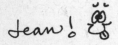

....

Dear God,

When I get hired for my next job, can You make
sure I don't get fired? I know I get unemployment ben-
efits from it, but still, it's kind of a drag.
Love,

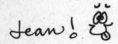

....

Dear God,

Thank you for keeping Hubby Rick safe on the afternoon of the tornado warnings. I know I wasn't very
happy when I found out that during those hours he
didn't call me, he wasn't missing at all, but riding out
the storms at Tacky's Tavern without bothering to call
me, even though I risked my life not going to the basement so my cell phone would still have reception. And
not only that, I found out that on that same day he

and his boneheaded buddy Craig actually tried to follow a funnel cloud in Rick's pickup truck. Like something out of the movie *Twister*. All I can say is thank You so much that You didn't make that funnel cloud touch down. But despite Rick's stupidity, I'm glad he was okay. I hope this also shows You that I'm a loving wife for being concerned.

Love,

Jean!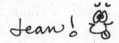

....

Dear God,

I'm not a vengeful person, as You know, but would it be asking too much if You maybe punished that snotty girl at the optical department at the Pamida? The one who today made me wait for forty minutes for my new eyeglasses while other customers got served within five minutes, and then sighed loudly when I asked her to loosen the temple pieces a little because they were too tight on my face? And then wouldn't take my $20-off coupon because it supposedly only extended to optical department purchases of $150.00 or more? What happened to "The customer is always right"? And aren't employees supposed to have sensitivity training for

dealing with customers who are not gorgeous (at least not the conventional definition of gorgeous)?

God, I'm not asking for anything severe or nasty, like death or third-degree burns, but could You push her down some stairs? Or break her nose? In case that's still too violent for Your peace-loving son Jesus' taste, how about sending down one of Your overweight angels (I'm sure You have them!) to visit her in a vision, and have it tell her to lay off her bad attitude at work, or when she dies she'll find herself in the hotter place! That would sure fix her wagon!

Love,

Jean!

Lovin' from Jean's Oven

No. 4:
Chocolate Bratwurst!

Imagine, a brat that tastes like chocolate! That's because it is chocolate! So delectable you'll wonder why you ate only the meat ones for so long! Hubby Rick actually tried one of my brats once (the only time he's eaten any of my chocolatey inventions!), and told me the next day that it was the only thing he's ever eaten that looked the exact same way coming out as it did going in! Hardee-har-har, Rick! (He's such a support!)

Ingredients:

3 oz. (three squares) unsweetened chocolate
²/₃ cup unsweetened cocoa

4 tbsp. butter
2 tbsp. whole milk
1 tsp. vanilla extract
1 egg
2¼ cups sugar
½ tsp. salt
1½ cups flour
extra cocoa
Optional extras: Croissants, brioche, waffles, or some
other rich, sweet-tasting bread; honey, butter, marshmallow creme, shredded coconut

Preheat your oven to 350° F if you like. Drop the
chocolate, cocoa, butter, and milk into a saucepan and
cook over low heat until it's all melted, stirring continuously. Set aside a few minutes to cool, then pour
mixture into a bowl, and add the vanilla, egg, sugar,
and salt. Mix with a wooden spoon until blended, then
add the flour and mix well until dough has a thick con-
sistency that makes it impossible to stir. This is your
bratwurst dough!

And now, the moment you've been waiting for—
time to get your hands dirty (and chocolatey)! Take a
ball of dough that fits in the palm of your hand, and
form it into a sausage shape about four inches long.

Roll the dough in a dish of loose cocoa so it gets coated all over. Place the dough about one inch apart on a greased baking sheet. Repeat until all

Arrange like this!

the dough is formed into sausages, and bake them for about 15–20 minutes, making sure they don't harden too much! Once out of the oven, re-roll the "bratwurst" in the cocoa, and cool.

When the bratwurst are cool, divide the croissants, brioche, or other bread in half, and insert each bratwurst between the halves to form individual sandwiches. For extra indulgence, mix ¼ cup honey with 3 tbsp. softened butter and spread the bread with it—that's your "mustard"! Or for you carb watchers, you can enjoy a chocolate bratwurst alongside some "potato salad" made out of marshmallow creme and toasted shredded coconut!

Excerpts from the Diary of Priscilla Teasdale

(Compiled with assistance from her mommy, Jean Teasdale!)

Dear Diary,

Ah, this is the life! This afternoon, I lay on the living room carpet, soaking up the sun's rays as they filtered through the sliding glass doors to our balcony! Sheer bliss! Then, natch, my bliss was interrupted by my goofy kitty brother Garfield, who just had to start chasing after the reflected bits of light from the sun-catcher Mommy Jean hung off one of the doors! How typical!

Dear Diary,

How I love living with my Mommy Jean! To her, we're not just (shudder) house pets! She treats my Garfield and me practically like we're her very own babies! She's very sensitive to our needs, too. It's like she's psychic! Don't ask me how she knows this, but she must have figured out that we get sick of our Meow Mix sometimes, because today Garf and me shared a yummy-nummy chicken parm sandwich Mommy brought home from the Italian deli. The Thousand Island dressing was the best! Then, the pièce de résistance: Ben & Jerry's Cherry Garcia ice cream! Our fave!

Dear Diary,

What a dream I just had! I dreamt that a mouse was racing around the house! I chased it and it disappeared under the refrigerator. Then it shot out from under the bed! I chased it some more. Finally, I cornered it in the shower stall! I was just about to get it when I heard the sound of laughter. My eyes snapped open, and I looked up in the direction of the sound. It

was Mommy Jean, giggling and filming me with her cell phone! I guess I was twitching in my sleep again. I love my Mommy Jean, but I wish no one had told her about YouTube!!

Dear Diary,

It's 3 a.m. A few minutes ago, I just coughed up a hairball the size of a snow globe on the bedroom carpet, next to the side of the bed where Mommy Jean is sleeping. Don't think I woke anyone with my retching. Oh, but look, Mommy Jean is getting up to use the bathroom!

Dear Diary,

I've been at it for years, I know, but I'm still trying to make a cat person out of my Daddy Rick! I'm forever trying to win his attention. I guess I like a challenge! Today, he was staring at that movement box again, while clicking on

the thing with buttons. His eyes fixed on the screen, sort of like how my eyes fix on a bird when it lands on our balcony. He was so rapt that he was sitting at the very edge of the sofa. When Daddy Rick acts like this, it's my cue to investigate!

I hopped on the couch next to him, and started rubbing against him. He nudged me with his elbow to get me to leave, but oh no, I'm too much of a veteran to be intimidated by that! Instead, I put my front paws on his leg, bent down, and started sniffing his fingers. Then I licked them! (Well, they tasted good! Sort of like seasoned popcorn salt!) After I did that, Daddy Rick jerked out of his seat and roared! That startled me. It's not like I meant to hurt him! Then he whirled around, lifted his forearm, and shoved me off the sofa. That sure wasn't very fatherly!

 As I quickly sprang atop my scratching tree, Daddy Rick yelled to Mommy Jean that I, Stupid Cat (Daddy Rick's special nickname for me), had caused him to lose his last life, just when he had almost won the level! I don't get it; he still looked alive to me!

I'm not sure why I rub Daddy Rick the wrong way. I must get to the bottom of it, though. Perhaps I'll finally solve the mystery tonight, when I sleep on his head!

Dear Diary,

I'd like to know why helping myself to a single piece of pepperoni off a whole pizza pie earns me a hard flick on my sweet little pink nose by Daddy Rick! It was just one teeny pepperoni. I guess Daddy Rick is just a big old meanie. The only time he ever interacts with me is when he plays this dumb tube sock game. He puts a tube sock over my head and laughs as I try to back out of it. It's not funny! It's hot and I can't breathe and I often end up smacking my head against a table leg. Once he did it to me when I was perched on the kitchen counter. I backed off the edge and tumbled several feet to the linoleum! I could've been seriously hurt!

It's funny, though: Even though she's much, much nicer, and never teases me, I tend to hiss at and scratch Mommy Jean more than Daddy Rick. I'm not sure why I act that way. In fact, Mommy constantly hugs and kisses me and cuddles me like a human baby! Maybe I'm just spoiled. Or maybe I just can't handle pure, un-adulterated bliss.

Wait, what am I doing? I'm a kitty—I don't have to explain myself! I just have to sit back and let the Meow Mix flow. All in all, things are pretty sweet here at Casa Teasdale!

More Jean Teasdale "Fun" Fiction!
Part 3: I Can Fly!

It was absolutely terrifying—at first. Surely this couldn't last. Yet, in spite of all the seemingly overwhelming odds, I wasn't dropping like a stone to the ground. Not even as the roofs and treetops got farther and farther beneath me. Gravity, my lack of feathers, or even my pleasant plumpness weren't preventing me from soaring into the wild blue yonder.

But it was true. Jean Teasdale, that silly gal everyone always underestimated, had liftoff.

I don't know what provoked me to climb to the roof of our apartment building. Normally my vertigo

would prevent me from such a stunt, but for some reason, heights weren't frightening me. Maybe it was the tough day at my new job, when my supervisor decided to extend my probationary period another two months because my cash register was negative ten bucks. Or maybe because my Ooey Gooey Choco-Cocoa-Mocha Cupcakes with Raspberry Filling and Coconut-Cream-Cheese-Cola Icing came out of the oven a little too ooey gooey. I just meant to get some air. Then I felt a rather brisk updraft whistling in my ears, and instinctively, I closed my eyes, felt the warmth of the sun on my head, and spread my windbreaker-clad arms outward. It was odd, as I had never really done anything like that before, but something about it felt right and soothing. I stood like that for what seemed like a minute or two, and when I eventually opened my eyes, I noticed my feet were dangling in midair, about a yard off the edge of the roof.

Jean Proverb #417

Sure, I look at the world through rose-colored glasses... Walmart had a sale on them!

Then I realized that my entire body hovered about a yard off the edge of the roof!

I tried to scramble back onto the roof, but the best I could do was drift towards it without

touching it. I was definitely airborne! A miracle! I lifted my arms and gently pumped them once, as if doing a breaststroke, and body responded by propelling forward and higher. Why was I chosen for such a great privilege and honor? I knew not why, but all I knew was, it was euphoric!

It didn't take long for people to notice. "There's a pleasantly plump woman flying up in the sky!" a man cried. Soon I was recognized. "It's a bird! It's a plane! It's Jean Teasdale, *The Onion*'s Humor and Human Interest columnist!" a woman shouted. "Oh, how I envy her, gamboling and banking like a carefree meadowlark!"

I didn't mean to be rude, but I was too full of joy to acknowledge them. Once in a while, in my dreams, I flew, but I always woke up on my familiar old waterbed, crushed that I had not actually taken wing at all. Now it was truly happening! Soon my fears melted away like a body ache dissolved by acetaminophen!

I continued to soar and spin about. I found that if I tilted to one side, I could roll over on my back and stare up at the blue sky! Putting my outstretched arms before me allowed me to descend. How fun it was to swoop and dive like a car on a roller coaster! The braver I became, the faster and more daring were my maneuvers! I did loop-de-loops and pirouettes and even tried

out some moves I saw on figure-skating programs. Underneath me, the thrilled gasps and shrieks of the stunned crowd below could be faintly heard.

Spreading my fingers out caused me to slow down a little, and lowering my legs and lifting my head up let me hover. My body responded to everything I did with great speed and efficiency—who knew all this time I was such a superb flying machine? The only time it didn't seem right was when I tried bobbing and weaving like a butterfly. I could do it, but the shaky fluttering made me a little nauseous, so I quickly put an end to that!

I never wanted to come down, even if it meant skipping dinner! As the sun began its descent, a chill appeared in the springtime breeze, but my shivers couldn't compete with the nearness of the gold-flecked clouds! I began to go higher...and higher...

A horn blasted through the noise below. It was the air horn from Hubby Rick's pickup truck. I'd know it anywhere. It startled me from my airborne reverie.

"How stupid!" I heard Rick shout. "Get down from there, Jean. You can't fly."

Couldn't fly? Well, that's precisely what I was doing, right? So how could he say that? I pretended to ignore him.

"What are you doing?" Rick yelled in that familiar growl of his. "Stop embarrassing yourself and come down. People are laughing at you."

I tried to hum to myself. "Theme from *Greatest American Hero*" was what came out. "Believe it or not, I'm walking on air...".

"Jean, you weigh far too much to be flying. Now come down here!" Rick bellowed.

Instinctively, I put my hands to my ears, but that caused me to jolt violently downward! My heart leaped. I tried my best to steady myself. I stopped my fall, but I was much lower to the ground. I looked down. The setting sun threw the horrified looks on people's faces into sharp, grotesque contrast. Rick wore his all-too-familiar expression of disgust.

Maybe Rick was right, I thought. I probably looked pretty silly and ungainly. Clearly I was disturbing the peace. What if I gave an old person a heart attack? What if I got arrested? I couldn't afford the bail. Seriously, who did I think I was?

At first I thought God had chosen me to fly so I could experience the heavenly rapture of flight. But maybe He was testing me on my limits. And I'd have to be pretty egotistical to deny them. After all, Rick and I were simple folk. We weren't ambitious, we didn't

have a lot of money, and let's face it, in the good-looking couples department, we were no John Tesh and Connie Sellecca. No, Jean Teasdale wasn't meant to fly. Certainly no more than anyone else, and possibly even less.

I plummeted. I turned somersaults and the wind rushed in my ears as I desperately clawed at the air. I tried to scream, but something vast and incredibly hard met me. Then all went black.

Sorry to end on such a down note (pun intended!). Also, sorry to use a tough word like "gamboling." I know this is meant to be a humor book. But I wanted to protest against closed-minded people (e.g. a certain chubby hubby) thinking that those who are in touch with their needs and dream of the impossible (e.g. yours truly) will never get anywhere in life. It's a metaphor. Or a simile. Some term like that.

THIS IS CRAP
IF JEAN FLEW ID
SELL HER TO THE CERCUS
—RICK

Recognizing Your
Limitations = Healthy

As I write this, I am in the middle of day two of one of my patented self-pity parties. (See the chapter called "Say It Loud and Proud—'I Feel Sorry for Myself!'" if you've been skipping around the book, which you are totally allowed to do, and don't get what I mean.) It began innocently enough as a mini-vacation from writing this book. I thought I'd take a nice short little break, get some housework done, pay some bills, clean out the litter box. Maybe even resume work on that frog hook rug with the staring eyes that I put aside last Easter.

I did wash some dishes. But as I was drying them and putting them away, I noticed that in the kitchen broom closet Hubby Rick had stuffed an enormous stash of potato chips, cheese curls, caramel popcorn,

beef jerky, Twizzlers, and two-liter bottles of Pepsi. Obviously he had stocked up for the upcoming football weekend. Normally these treats are off-limits to the football widow (a.k.a. me!), but there was so much more than usual that I figured he wouldn't care if I snagged one or two bags of everything. After all, writing gives me a big appetite (right up there with breathing and hearing!), and it would save me a trip to the grocery store. So I took them into the bedroom, changed into a fresh, clean sleep-shirt and socks, sacked out on the waterbed, and grabbed the remote control. Within minutes I was feeling sorry for myself, and lo, here I still am, thirty-six hours later and counting!

I never intended to close *A Book of Jean's Own!* with a self-pity party. But I never not intended to, either! Think about it—here I am, writing my first-ever book, under a back-breaking deadline, and I'm completely and utterly tapped out. I figured being a first-time author would be both a walk in the park and a piece of cake, but turns out I'm not very good at walking and eating at the same time! (Okay, almost tapped out. I admit that was pretty funny.)

I must confess, at this point I'm feeling more than a little exploited. How am I supposed to make fun,

wacky observations about life and stuff if I'm constantly chained to my word processor and not experiencing
life? Maybe everyone thinks Jean Teasdale is just some
cash cow they can milk, but you don't see me mooing
along in agreement! I would never, ever think to put
this kind of pressure on anyone else—why are they demanding the world of me?

Sure, I suppose they expect me to be grateful that
they trusted me to produce a book. But have they ever
tried to walk in my fuzzy slippers? You may think it's
all gumdrops and peppermints being Jean Teasdale,
but think again. In actuality, as I go about my daily
life, I put up with a lot of jealousy from others. That's
right, jealousy! There's more than one grouch in this
world who envies my sunny, funny, happy-go-lucky de-
meanor and immediately has to try to pounce on it and
rip it to shreds!

Need proof? Last week, when I was taking a break
from writing to go grocery shopping, a woman sidled up
to me in the Pamida parking lot and said "Still wearing your P.J.s, huh?" then casually strolled away. I was
so taken aback that I stopped dead in my tracks and
couldn't respond. What left me speechless was not the
fact that she mystifyingly mistook for a pajama outfit
what were obviously a pair of fresh-from-the-dryer pink

velour sweatpants, a yellow cotton top silk-screened with a basket of sleeping kittens, and my comfiest wool clogs. Instead, she actually thought she had the right to go up to a total stranger and make a negative remark about her appearance. I mean, who does that? I can only chalk up such behavior to the green-eyed monster. Tear someone down by distorting her most winning qualities as things to be ridiculed. I'm convinced that this explains why I've never gotten far in my career. I try so hard to please, only to hear at my six-month evaluation that my work performance is sloppy and I pester the other employees, so I'd better shape up or ship out. I know I'm in the right in these situations, but this constant stubborn resistance can really wear you down.

At heart, I'm just a simple person who needs her leisure. After a long four hours at my current job at the indoor flea market, I just want to come home to two cats that love me, a Polarfleece afghan that's calling my name, a DVR full of that day's soaps, and Fabio in an apron taking a chocolate soufflé out of the oven. Okay, maybe that last one is a bit of a stretch. I'd gladly accept Mark Harmon! Kidding! But seriously, if baby doesn't get some quality time, baby gets cranky, and that's when baby digs in her heels!

Of course I know my editor keeps leaving increasingly desperate messages on my voicemail. Of course I can hear Hubby Rick yelling at me. I'm not ignoring them—I'm acknowledging them. At least, I'm acknowledging them silently. I'm just not letting them get to me. They want an overworked Jean Teasdale on the verge of mental and physical collapse. See, that's what the normal, dreary, everyday world demands of everyone, to work until they drop. But I refuse to buy into this mindlessness. It's vital to stop and smell the roses. Or in my case, the empty Twizzler bag (which has traces of a lovely strawberry scent).

Yet, in a very profound way, Jeanketeers, my self-pity party symbolizes the triumph of the human spirit. I am not letting the weight of this book crush me! Instead, I am just shrugging it off and letting go. Isn't that the most beautiful, soothing, and downright liberating thing you've ever heard? After all, don't the know-it-alls on morning TV tell us that recognizing your limitations is healthy?

Today marks the birth of a whole new Jean Teasdale! A Jean who no longer tries to do it all and be everything to everyone! A Jean who acknowledges, hey,

maybe I just wasn't meant to be an author, and you know what? That's totally, one hundred percent okay! I feel great! Why didn't I have this epiphany sooner?

Well, world, I am hereby spreading my limited wings and proclaiming my limitations. My name is Jean Teasdale, and I am limited. Hear me, world? I am limited! I am limited!

I am limited! I am limited! I am limited! I am limited! I am limited! I am limited! I am limited! I am limited! I am limited! I am limited! I am limited! I am limited! I am limited! I am limited! I am limited! I am limited! I am limited! I am limited! I am limited! I am limited!

I am limited! I am limited!

I am limited! I am limited! I am limited! I am limited! I am limited! I am limited! I am limited! I am limited! I am limited! I am limited! I am limited! I am

limited! I am limited!

I am limited! I am limited!

I am limited! I am limited! I am limited! I am limited! I am limited! I am limited! I am limited! I am limited! I am limited! I am limited! I am limited! I am limited! I am limited! I am limited! I am limited! I am limited! I am

limited! I am limited! I am limited! I am limited! I am
limited! I am limited! I am limited! I am limited! I am
limited! I am limited! I am limited! I am limited! I am
limited! I am limited! I am limited! I am limited! I am
limited! I am limited! I am limited! I am limited! I am
limited! I am limited! I am limited! I am limited! I am
limited! I am limited! I am limited! I am limited! I am
limited! I am limited! I am limited! I am limited! I am
limited! I am limited! I am limited! I am limited! I am
limited! I am limited! I am limited! I am limited! I am
limited! I am limited! I am limited! I am limited! I am
limited! I am limited! I am limited! I am limited! I am
limited! I am limited! I am limited! I am limited! I am
limited!

I am limited! I am limited! I am limited! I am lim-
ited! I am limited! I am limited! I am limited! I am
limited! I am limited! I am limited! I am limited! I am
limited! I am limited! I am limited! I am limited! I am
limited! I am limited! I am limited! I am limited! I am
limited! I am limited! I am limited! I am limited! I am
limited! I am limited! I am limited! I am limited! I am
limited! I am limited! I am limited! I am limited! I am
limited! I am limited! I am limited! I am limited! I am
limited! I am limited! I am limited! I am limited! I am
limited! I am limited! I am limited! I am limited! I am

limited! I am limited! I am

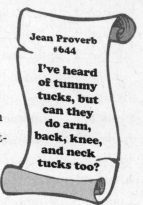

Jean Proverb #644

I've heard of tummy tucks, but can they do arm, back, knee, and neck tucks too?

limited! I am limited!

I am limited! I am

limited! I am limited!

I am limited! I am limited!...

[Editor's Note: This chapter, which was received in longhand on ruled notebook paper, continues on in this manner for eight more pages.]

Hubby Rick to the Rescue

Knew Id have to bail the broad out in some way.

I dont write, hate writing, hate readng. writting & books for winers. winers like Jean. WRITING=GAY but I have to write this book now cuz shes hours away from her whatever, due time. and shes locked in the bedroom and says shes all done 7& tired out 7& the world can suck a fart. Shit if she said this before she got 6his book job I would of rispected that, But now shes in a fix cuz she bit off more 5han she can chew. & wer'e getting calls from some b0ok guy and this screchy bitch Judeth from the0nnion saying send th6 rest of the chaptars she owes us. Guess theyneeded them days ago. shit how familar. these suckers didnt no what they were geting into. and Jean does she want her stuped cats to die or somthing. Cuz they been screming

for food 7& no way am I tking care of the litle fartbags. Shit yu not 1 farts like a fertalizer factory. I got the rest of thisbook thing to write. And I cant even typ3

0K homos, where were we. Where did Jena leve off. seeing somthing here in a notebook, a bunch of prov3rbs. .... Oh hell no Im not typeing down this lame shit.Heres some provrbs of mine. all you need to know. same shit diffrent day. Lifes a bitch 7& then you die. if your waiting forsomething meningfull to come out of awoman and y0ur looking at her mouth your looking at the wrong end.--That last one is for the Judth broad at The onon.

Seeing some ricepes too. christ That gross choclate stuff she makes. 0K so heres a recpe. Take two fat shits, & see if any one cares. oh you wanted a real r3cipe. my mistake fags. 0K Take some brats 8& boil them in beer Then take some saltene crackrs and butter them. There you g0. Dinner. that was hard.

Cat diary—Jesus Crist 0K heres a cat diry. cat sleept all day, ate and shat in abox. Repeat a million times. The End.

And stop caling me Hubby Rick dipshits. Its just Rick or Teasdale no hubby. If you want your ass laid 0ut with a tireiron keep saying Hubby Rick Huby RicK

&&^%8473fgeela Fuckfuckfuck this typeing shit.

FUCK SENTENCES Im thru Im talk into a tape re-
crder & some looser with no life can take it all down

[Tape begins]

Okay, so I finally found the damn tape recorder and
I'm recording or whatever now. So yeah, Jean dropped
the ball big-time, no big surprise. She never finishes
nothing. Now she's all mopey poor-little-me. I mean,
she must come out to take a dump once in a while, but
I ain't catched her yet. I ain't seen her for days, 'cause
I gotta go out and work a job, you know, a real job? The
kind you spend nine hours working your ass off at and
get shitfaced afterwards? Anyhow. Bedroom blinds are
closed and the windows are shut so I bet it's getting
pretty ripe in there. Shit, even talking into a tape recorder is gay. It's like I'm talking to myself like a crazy.
Jean better appreciate what I'm doing for her, do you
hear me Jean? I'm saving your damn book! I better
get a big cut! Especially since you're eating my football
snacks! Seriously, what the hell? They're all missing
from the kitchen cabinet! Dammit, Jean, I told you stay
away from my snacks!

[Rustling sounds, unintelligible speaking]

Okay, well, she already ate some of my snacks. This isn't the first time Jean has pulled crap like this. Once we were watching CNN and she saw herself on screen and got all "Boo hoo hoo, poor me." I guess some camera guys were taking shots of fat-asses at the mall and they shot Jean and it wound up on the news. Only shots from the neck down, you didn't see the faces. Still I could pick her out right away. She was wearing this pink crap with a Minnie Mouse on it. No mistaking it.

Well, I wanted to make her feel better, so I laughed. It was pretty funny. I mean, she is a fat-ass. And it's not like they showed her face. Only her and me knew who it really was. It was really no big deal. But after I laughed she stopped moaning and stared at me with this weird look on her face. Then she got up from the couch and walked real slow to the bedroom. I thought maybe she was feeling better and wanted to fool around or something. So I get up and follow her and I try to put my arm around her, but she shoves it away, and slams the door and locks me out. I'm telling you, I didn't see the inside of that bedroom for four straight days. She only came out when I threatened to give the cats to science. I should try that again. The woman's a wack job. I should take the doorknob out of the door so she can't lock the door no more. And padlock the snacks.

Maybe I handled the TV thing wrong. Maybe I should of said something nice after I laughed. But how the hell am I supposed to know what she's thinking. Jesus, women! I mean, if you're fat, face the truth. If you ain't gonna do anything about it, own it. Take some damn responsibility. I'm fat, and I'm gonna stay that way, cause ain't no way I'm gonna eat hippie rabbit food ever. I don't give a two-handed fuck what anyone thinks about me. I been called all the names in the book: fat, fatso, asshole, dumbass, shithead, piece of shit, shit-for-brains, shitpile, shitstain, shitbag, shitlicker, shitfucker, shitdropper, shitadmiral, whatever. What mattered is that I pissed someone off, and it felt real, real good. Whatever someone thinks of you, good or bad, is their own goddamn problem.

What else. Yeah, Jean's weird. Aw hell, I'll never get that broad. She was always off-the-wall, even in high school. She'd go around in, like, Mork suspenders, years after it went off the air. No one did that any more, not even those boat people kids who came to our school after being kicked out of Chong Chop Chang or whatever and always wore out-of-style shit. I used to hang out with her older brother Kevin all the time and even he said she was a few bricks shy of a load, and this was a guy who used to light his farts in broad daylight to impress

chicks. He drove with his knees. Still can't believe he got Jesus, man. I started hanging out with Jean not 'cause I wanted to, but 'cause I was best buds with Kevin. And you know, underneath those huge glasses and weirdo pigtails and stupid watermelon lip gloss she was always smearing on, she wasn't all that bad-looking. Back then she weighed 100 pounds less, even though she was still kind of chunky. But I couldn't help liking her, you know? For one thing, she didn't go around acting like she had a cinder block pounded up her ass like most of the chicks at school. She was always smiling and shit. That could make you feel good sometimes.

At first, I thought she would be easy, because she was starving for attention. And you know how girls are about first boyfriends, especially the hardcases who don't normally get dates. But turned out I had to bide my time a little.

[Belches]

Not cause she was a bitch though. She just didn't want anyone busting her hole right away. But I liked that. It meant we could just hang out and go to a movie or the batting cages or whatever with no pressure. Even though I really wanted to get laid, it was kind of a re-

lief at the same time. It was like she was classy. Well, classy isn't the right word. A virgin. Yeah, that's it. And when we did finally do it, she was a crier. Normally that would have had me heading for the nearest state line, but for some reason it was kind of sweet. She still cries by the way. Now it's weird.

Can't tell you how many times I wished our parents never caught us in my pickup at the Jewel parking lot and made us get hitched. Then I think about what Jean's got other than me: a bitch-on-wheels for a mom, a Christ-bitten killjoy of a brother, a stuck-up stepsister who never calls, and a lunatic dad who dresses up like Santa. Plus a couple of cats who just stare at her. Her only friend is this flaky homo who gave her this stupid flea market job that pays shit. The broad has so many strikes against her—who the hell else is going to look after her?

If you Jeanketeers, if there even is such a thing, believe any of that crap Jean probably tells you about me not supporting her, then you're bigger losers than I thought. While Jean sits around and mopes and thinks about herself and loses jobs and pretends her cats like her and writes it all down in her stupid column, I work and pay the bills and make it possible for her to dick around. Whatever. It's her damn thing, I leave her to

it. I don't pretend to understand or care about it. But I wouldn't take it away from her because it means a lot to her, even if she's crapping out on it right now.

[Belches]

Plus you should see some of the pieces of work my friends have balled. My buddy Craig once had this girlfriend who was a perfect ten, no shit. But it turned out she was even more nutso than Jean, and I know this because I don't got no scars on the back of my skull from where a carpenter's plane bounced off blade-side first. Catch my drift? Jesus, when do I ever say "catch my drift"? I'm telling you, it's talking into this tape recorder that's the problem. It makes you say gay things.

Where was I? Oh yeah. Jean's nutso, but she ain't psycho-evil nutso. Overall, she ain't so bad. She drives me crazy with all her cat and stuffed-animal crap and her clinging and wanting a baby—Jesus, that's a whole other thing—but at least she puts a little, I don't know, softness into my life. Otherwise I'd probably be eating Taco Bell off oil pans instead of plates with flowers on them. Though I don't see what it hurts to pee in the shower. Still, even with all the craziness, I'd rather have Jean around than not around, I guess. Not like I could

do any better. But I could do a lot worse. Oh shit I sound like a pussy now. How do you rewind this? Fucker.

[Rustling sounds, cursing, sound of glass breaking, more cursing]

Know what, I'm through. This is the last fucking time I ever do anything for a book. Seriously, I can see how this book-writing can turn you into Oprah. You have to think and act all sensitive and shit and impress a bunch of idiots you're never going to meet anyway. Fuck that. Look, whoever prints this book, don't include that mushy stuff I said before. Just take it out. Only keep in the parts about me not giving a shit about what others think and where Craig's psycho ex threw a carpenter's plane at him. See, if Jean wants to be a real writer and write stuff people will actually read, she should do up some of those *Penthouse* letters. I'd even help her with the terms and stuff. At least she'd get paid good for it. But for now, at least buy her book so we can get some cash. Okay, that's all. Oh, and go Vikes! Vikings ruuuuuuule!

[Several seconds of guttural bellowing and lowing. Tape ends]

Keep Smiling!

I'm baaaa-aaaack, Jeanketeers! (Did you miss me?) Sorry if you found my li'l mental vaycay a bit jolting. But believe it or not, it did wonders! Now that I'm nearly done with this book, my mind is as clear as a bell again! Turns out there was light at the end of the tunnel, and I needn't have worried a bit!

Before I recount my glorious comeback, I wanted to apologize on behalf of Hubby Rick for all that swearing in the last chapter. I am real, real sorry about his disgusting vulgarity. I'm sure it was an awful shock to everyone who picked up this book for some lighthearted and gently madcap humor. But what

NOBEL PEACE PRIZE!

← chocolate-filled!

1ST PLACE: Jean Teasdale!

can I say, that's the hubby for you. Why I haven't been awarded the Nobel Peace Prize for putting up with all that for my entire adult life, I'll never know! I think Rick permanently keeps his mind in—well, I don't want to compound his grossness, so let's just say he keeps it in that area under the couch cushions that I always forget to vacuum. (That's less gross than saying the container that the toilet brush sits in.)

As for the few other words between the cursing, suffice it to say that I very much disagree with all of them! If he didn't pay the rent, Rick would find himself in the doghouse pronto! I'd offer a rebuttal, but I wouldn't know where to start, and I don't wish to end on a sour note. (But I will say that I haven't cried after whoopee for years! What udder cow-chips! Rick is confusing crying with staring at the ceiling. Two entirely different things, obviously.)

So I took a little unexpected time off from the book. It was completely spontaneous and unplanned. Day and night, I lay adrift on my waterbed, wearing my Tweety Bird nightshirt and one pink sock (not sure what happened to the other one). My world had shrunken down to half a tub of caramel popcorn, several two-liter bottles of Pepsi, and reruns of *Bridezillas* (one of whom I still aspire to be someday). In short, the

self-pity party was in full swing, and it was the best I had ever thrown. Yes, I had snapped, but it felt great. Abandoning my responsibilities had never felt so relaxing! I could have lay there forever, floating, floating, floating, my life but a dream.

The fourth day rolled around. Or maybe it was the fifth day. Hubby Rick was shouting at me behind the bedroom door as usual. This time he said something about a phone message. I just put my pillow over my head. About half an hour later, I heard a rapping at my bedroom window. I tried to pretend I couldn't hear it, but the darn rapping wouldn't stop, so after a couple minutes I roused myself from bed (no easy feat) and raised the blind. Directly out the window, just inches from the windowpane, hovered the receiver to our living room cordless phone. It had been crudely duct-taped to a wooden yardstick, which in turn was duct-taped to a broken car radio antenna. The contraption was coming from the direction of the balcony that adjoins our living room. I opened the window.

A loud click sounded on the receiver; the speaker-phone function had been switched on to the maximum volume level. A male voice said my name. He gave his name and said he was an attorney for Onion Books. He said that I was in clear violation of the terms of

my publishing contract, and if I did not produce a full manuscript within twenty-four hours, I would be sued for breach of contract. A click, then silence. Then I heard another beep, and the message began again. The message repeated several more times before I finally emerged from the bedroom and yanked Rick back into the living room, causing him to nearly drop the phone, yardstick, and all.

And that's exactly where I am right now, Jeanketeers! Nestled cozily among my trusty, familiar knickknacks, potpourri, throw pillows, and two beloved flabby tabbies, I am once again pecking at my trusty old Dell, putting the finishing touches on the very book that you are holding!

You see, even though my self-pity party had its good moments throughout, I wasn't truthfully living up to my own personal axiom—"Keep Smiling!" After all, as we all know so well, life is not perfect. In everyone's lives, one or two instances of challenge or hardship occur. (Occasionally more, though it's rare.) But when we're faced with adversity, running away from it is not always an option, so we must do our best to face it. We're all in it together, so instead of being Debbie Deniers, we should shrug, smile, and see those bad times through.

So I pinned the smiley-face button back on my soul, put my shoulder to the grindstone, and got back to work. Now, for the very first time in my life, I, Jean Teasdale, am finally fulfilling one of my very biggest and most heartfelt dreams. One possibly even bigger and more heartfelt than becoming a Mommy. I'm finishing something I set out to accomplish. It's not just vacuuming out my car or completing a hook rug with a frog with staring eyes on it. It's writing the final chapter of my very first book. And if that isn't the most life-affirming thing you ever heard, well, drop me an email and tell me what is, because I'd sure like to find out!

I hope that my example inspires you, too. I'm soooo glad that in addition to making you giggle until you puddled your pantaloons, which I'll go ahead and assume I did, I may have given you the idea to pursue your own lifelong dream and turn it into wonderful, sparkling reality. And if you should stall or fail to follow through, maybe you'll even be as lucky as me and be given a huge incentive to finish, like the threat of a big fat breach-of-contract suit.

And even if you have absolutely zero going on in your life and it's likely to stay that way, I hope you at least take a hint from your pal Jean and realize how important it is to keep smiling, no matter what life

throws at you! We have to find reasons to smile and laugh and savor those special moments both large and small. We mustn't take our time on Earth for granted, for we only have one life that we know of, and it's a short one. (Well, except for mine. I really believe I'm going to live to at least 110! Don't know why exactly, I just feel it. I have a really positive attitude, which helps. Also, by rarely walking and never exercising, I conserve a lot of energy, so I'm hoping it will take longer to use up.)

Index

G

H

J

K

L

M

T

Look for These Upcoming Humor Titles by Jean Teasdale from Onion Books!

The Boss Who Could Have Been My ~~Teenage Son~~ Slightly Younger Brother: Adventures (And Misadventures!) in Minimum-Wage Employment

That's Not Something Out of the Litter Box, That's My Choco-Cherry-Peppermint-Hazelnut Brownies! Kitchen Follies with Jean Teasdale

Teasdale on Teasdale: Reflections on Life with a Chubby, Grubby Hubby

Are Those Sloppy Joes, or a Mad Scientist Experiment? More Kitchen Follies with Jean Teasdale

Priscilla Teasdale's Kitty Letters to God

Is That Peanut Butter in Your Diaper?!? And Other Crazy Stuff that Might Happen If I Ever Become a Mother!

Maria Schneider is Jean Teasdale's brain.
Chapter design by Rick Martin.
Lisa Pompilio designed the cover.
Interior photos by Mike Faisca and Nick Gallo.
Copy editing by Rebecca Bengal.